Decentralized Energy

AAAS Selected Symposia Series

Published by Westview Press, Inc.
5500 Central Avenue, Boulder, Colorado

for the

American Association for the Advancement of Science
1776 Massachusetts Avenue, N.W., Washington, D.C.

Decentralized Energy

Edited by Paul P. Craig
and Mark D. Levine

Routledge
Taylor & Francis Group
LONDON AND NEW YORK

First published 1982 by Westview Press

Published 2018 by Routledge
52 Vanderbilt Avenue, New York, NY 10017
2 Park Square, Milton Park, Abingdon, Oxon OX14 4RN

Routledge is an imprint of the Taylor & Francis Group, an informa business

Library of Congress Catalog Card Number 82-50869
ISBN 0-86531-407-l

ISBN 13: 978-0-367-01937-2 (hbk)
ISBN 13: 978-0-367-16924-4 (pbk)

About the Book

The question of decentralization of energy sources goes to the heart of the energy choices before the United States, but conflicting viewpoints have clouded the issue in recent years. This volume cuts through the rhetoric to address specific issues involving local control over energy sources and energy uses, including environmental aspects of decentralized and centralized energy supply systems; energy conservation and its relation to energy decentralization; behavior, values, and energy choices; institutional issues affecting the commercialization of solar energy, especially in cities; issues of decentralized and conventional energy supply choices in Sweden; and methods by which decentralized energy systems have been studied. Most importantly, each of the papers in this collection considers social and institutional concerns as well as technical and economic issues.

About the Series

The *AAAS Selected Symposia Series* was begun in 1977 to provide a means for more permanently recording and more widely disseminating some of the valuable material which is discussed at the AAAS Annual National Meetings. The volumes in this *Series* are based on symposia held at the Meetings which address topics of current and continuing significance, both within and among the sciences, and in the areas in which science and technology impact on public policy. The *Series* format is designed to provide for rapid dissemination of information, so the papers are not typeset but are reproduced directly from the camera-copy submitted by the authors. The papers are organized and edited by the symposium arrangers who then become the editors of the various volumes. Most papers published in this *Series* are original contributions which have not been previously published, although in some cases additional papers from other sources have been added by an editor to provide a more comprehensive view of a particular topic. Symposia may be reports of new research or reviews of established work, particularly work of an interdisciplinary nature, since the AAAS Annual Meetings typically embrace the full range of the sciences and their societal implications.

WILLIAM D. CAREY
Executive Officer
American Association for
the Advancement of Science

Contents

About the Editors and Authors

Paul P. Craig, *a physicist by training, is professor of applied science at the University of California, Davis. A specialist in energy policy, he served as vice chairman of the Biennial Report Advisory Committee, California Energy Commission, and as energy advisor to the Science Advisor to the President (1973-1975). He has more than 100 publications in physics, energy policy, and conservation.*

Mark D. Levine *is a policy analyst in the Energy and Environment Division at Lawrence Berkeley Laboratory in Berkeley, California. Currently he is principal investigator of projects to develop energy performance standards for residential and commercial buildings; to develop energy efficiency standards for residential appliances, including heating and cooling equipment; and to develop engineering and economic studies of energy conservation.*

Steven Ferrey, *senior energy counsel, National Consumer Law Center, Boston, Massachusetts, is a specialist in energy law and policy, with a particular interest in conservation and renewable energy financing and applications. He has served as a member of the President's Domestic Policy Review on Solar Energy and on the Office of Technology Assessment's Cogeneration Advisory Board. Some solutions to the problems outlined in this volume are discussed in his most recent publication, "Solar Banking: New Solutions to the Urban Energy Crisis"* (Harvard Journal on Legislation, *vol. 18, no. 3, summer 1981).*

Luther P. Gerlach, *professor of anthropology at the University of Minnesota, Minneapolis, is concerned with social movements and change, social factors in resource development and human ecology. He has written on energy conflicts, on our evolving energy interdependence, and on the key leverage factors in technology delivery systems for solar heating and cooling.*

John P. Holdren *is professor of energy and resources at the University of California, Berkeley, a principal investigator for the Energy and Environment Division, Lawrence Berkeley Laboratory, and a faculty consultant to the Magnetic Fusion Energy Division, Lawrence Livermore Laboratory. He has written or edited numerous publications on energy technology and policy, environmental problems, and population, among them* Ecoscience: Population, Resources, Environment *(with P.R. Ehrlich et al.; W.H. Freeman, 1977) and* Global Ecology *(edited with P.R. Ehrlich; Harcourt Brace Jovanovich, 1971), and he has served on the National Academy of Sciences' Committee on Nuclear and Alternative Energy Systems.*

Clifton Hores, *a policy analyst for the Tosco Foundation in Boulder, Colorado, has specialized in energy management and policy evaluation for local governments. Currently he is involved in a project to evaluate the socioeconomic consequences of energy development in the Rocky Mountain region.*

Barry Hyman *is associate professor and director of the Program in Social Management of Technology at the University of Washington, Seattle. He was staff engineer for the U.S. Senate Commerce Committee, working on energy policy issues, and he was project director and editor of* Decentralized Electricity for Washington, *a project sponsored by the Ford Foundation.*

Thomas B. Johansson *is associate professor in the Environmental Studies Program at the University of Lund, Sweden. His publications include* Solar Sweden *(with P. Steen; Stockholm: Secretariat for Futures Studies, 1978),* Solar Versus Nuclear: Choosing Energy Futures *(with P. Steen and M. Lönnroth; Pergamon, 1980), and* Energy in Transition: A Report on Energy Policy and Future Options *(with P. Steen and M. Lönnroth) and* Radioactive Waste from Nuclear Power Plants *(with P. Steen; University of California Press, 1980 and 1981, respectively).*

Måns Lönnroth *is at the Secretariat for Futures Studies in Stockholm, Sweden. A specialist in energy and social organization, he is the author of* Energy in Transition: A Report on Energy Policy and Future Options *(with T.B. Johansson and P. Steen; University of California Press, 1980) and* Solar Versus Nuclear: Choosing Energy Futures *(with P. Steen and T.B. Johansson; Pergamon, 1980).*

Peter Steen *is head of the Systems Analysis Division at the Swedish Defence Research Institute in Stockholm. His publications include* Solar Sweden *(with T.B. Johansson; Stockholm: Secretariat for Futures Studies, 1978),* Solar

Versus Nuclear: Choosing Energy Futures *(with M. Lönnroth and T.B. Johansson; Pergamon, 1980), and* Energy in Transition: A Report on Energy Policy and Future Options *(with M. Lönnroth and T.B. Johansson) and* Radioactive Waste from Nuclear Power Plants *(with T.B. Johansson; University of California Press, 1980 and 1981, respectively).*

Paul P. Craig, Mark D. Levine

Introduction

We live in an era in which perceptions of directions and goals are even more important than the techniques used to achieve these goals. Things have not always been so. In earlier times (and in many parts of the world today), there were such severe limits on simply obtaining the necessities of life that the opportunity for choice was severely circumscribed. Today, in the industrialized regions of the West, we live in an era of extreme abundance, and this provides us with a flexibility which simply did not previously exist. The consequences are being seen throughout the developed world: from the ennui and loss of direction so characteristic of United States youth (and many adults as well) to the spirit of rebellion which keeps recurring even in controlled nations such as Poland.

There are rapid shifts in the loci of power. For example, consider the energy sector. At one time, the electric utilities could make decisions alone on need for new facilities and how to finance them. They could then go into the capital market and raise money. Utility stocks were considered secure - the stable core of the American capitalistic system; the utility stocks were for folks planning to retire and who wanted secure investments with ample return. No longer. Today utilities are valued by the market at well below book value, and are generally considered risky, particularly in the aftermath of Three Mile Island. Utilities once had control over facility siting. Today this sense of control has evaporated. Utilities can propose sites, but much of the decision making authority resides elsewhere. This "elsewhere" is not always so clear. Even where there exist "one-stop" agencies to approve new facilities, there are many actors. Regulatory agencies may suffer from internal division which makes the life of commissioners and staff members very difficult. (This is the case with the California Energy Commission, a "one-stop" plan which has not succeeded). There are a multiplicity of agencies, each with its own staff and its own constituency. There are environmental groups, trade groups, business groups, political subgroups, and labor groups which are prepared to litigate if their voices are not heard. The cries of anguish from the energy industries, as their power erodes, are heard loud in the land. Think of the Mobil Oil Corporation Sunday morning ads in Parade Magazine and many newspapers. Here is a company that clearly thinks it knows the answers, but people are not accepting them as they once did.

These changes in the working environment of business are reflective of profound changes taking place in our value system. More accurately, they are a specific consequence of a major reexamination of goals and values, which may turn out to be one of the most important aspects of the latter third of the twentieth century. The papers in this volume represent a set of viewpoints on one side of this multifaceted reexamination. While we cannot here attempt to fully characterize such a profound process as we believe to be taking place, we can provide some perspectives on outlooks.

The differences in perspective are caught especially clearly in a review article of three energy futures studies by Paul Joskow (1980) in the Bell Journal of Economics and in one of René Dupos "Despairing Optimist" columns in The American Scholar (1980). Joskow reviews the three major energy futures studies published in the last year (Stobaugh, 1979; Ford Foundation, 1979; and RFF, 1979). The latter two studies are firmly anchored in the viewpoint that if the economic system is unfettered, America and the world can solve the energy problem. The Harvard (Stobaugh) report is less sanguine about the market solving all problems; it suggests an emphasis on solar energy and conservation as the keys to the future. Joskow, an economics professor at Harvard and MIT, comes down firmly on the side of free enterprise. He concludes his discussion with his wish "that the blueprint established in the Ford study would become a guide for public policy in the United States."

The Ford study is, in essence, a brief for turning the market system free. Values, which are never made explicit, are clearly derived from Adam Smith. The key recommendations of the Ford report are summarized by Joskow as follows:

(1) Energy prices should be allowed to rise freely to reflect the opportunity cost of energy to the U.S. economy. The government should exit from the price regulation/product allocation business.

(2) Flexible, economic mechanisms should be used to "internalize" externalities, such as pollution, so that the costs of alternative energy sources reflect the full social cost of utilization. The government should define basic pollution standards, but not establish rigid and detailed source-specific technological, cleanup, or emissions standards.

(3) As a general matter, decentralized market mechanisms should be used instead of detailed unworkable government regulations and bureaucratic production, consumption, and fuel-utilization criteria.

(4) Government should focus less on demonstration and deployment of a small number of large technological projects and more on basic research aimed at defining a wide array of opportunities and generic information useful for many technological applications. The private sector should be relied on to the greatest extent in the development, demonstration, and deployment of specific technologies. More basic scientific research, and less "commercial hardware" research, is needed.

(5) Where energy prices are kept below the social opportunity cost of consumption, or where market imperfections lead to incorrect decisions, government intervention in the form of subsidies, information, and technical assistance, moral suasion, etc., should be encouraged. However, these activities should be undertaken only after careful consideration of the cost effectiveness of the form of intervention. As a general matter, the group frowns on large subsidies and thinks that they should be used only where there is a clear indication that market mechanisms do not work well, and then only to the extent necessary to "simulate" what a smoothly functioning market would do.

(6) We have two interrelated energy problems. The first, a long-term problem, is to learn to adapt efficiently to higher energy prices. The second is to position ourselves to respond to sudden "shocks" in ways that cushion the economy from such shocks as much as possible. The general conclusion is that government has not only performed poorly in structuring policies to achieve these ends, but that the policies adopted are actually counterproductive.

Contrast this view with that of Dubos.

> Purely technical solutions, however, do not contribute much to peace and happiness if we do not know how to deal with the more human aspects of life - for example, unemployment or the degrading poverty that prevails over immense areas of the globe.

The free market economists might respond to this concern by observing that we need technologies to overcome these problems, and that a reduction of constraints on the economic system will move us toward solutions. Dubos would disagree. In his view we have (or can create) enough technology; our problem is how to put it to work in the service of mankind:

> Surveys carried out in several prosperous countries, including Japan, reveal that a very large percentage of people are now less interested in the acquisition of wealth than in simpler ways of life, more leisure, and greater personal freedom. Once a reasonable level of affluence has been achieved, it seems certain that further increase does not result in better health or greater happiness. However, many people, even in prosperous countries, believe that they have yet to reach the ideal level, and probably the great majority of people in the Third World are eager to achieve the kind of prosperity that some of us have begun, or pretend, to disdain.
>
> Although the future cannot be predicted, certain forces or trends that are common in the modern world may justify the hope that human life can be improved without creating the problems that have so far resulted from economic success. I realize that my view of these trends is contaminated with a great deal of wishful thinking, but I shall nevertheless suggest that money may not continue to be the ultimate criterion of wealth because the nonmaterial aspects of life seem to be becoming increasingly important in the personal and even national calculations of success.
>
> Schumacher's phrase "Small is beautiful" achieved such rapid and widespread acceptance and popularity that it must correspond to some deep human longing, in particular to a desire for greater simplicity and decentralization. Most people feel that institutions must be reorganized on a more human scale so that they can be more readily comprehended by the human mind. It was believed a generation ago that the world was becoming a global village in which all human life would be homogenized, but there is now a marked trend in the opposite direction. Local regions are preferred to large countries; moderate-sized towns grow, whereas some huge urban agglomerations have

begun to shrink; small shops and boutiques have become more numerous; the work of artisans and folk celebrations are increasingly fashionable.

In proposing to the AAAS a session on decentralization we began from a position of support for many of the ideas expressed by Professor Dubos. Economics alone, without a road map, cannot be expected to resolve our energy dilemma. A sense of direction is needed. We are a wealthy nation, and have the resources to select any of a large number of technically feasible paths. The coming decades will see a continuing debate over the proper balance, and over the choice of technical and social systems. It is our belief that these choices offer us an important opportunity to develop energy systems capable of expanding human freedom and individuation. The evolution of new institutions is even harder than the development of new technologies. In terms of human satisfaction it is also far more important.

It is our hope that the papers presented in this volume will prove of help to those attempting to understand this complex scene. As symposium convenors, we take no position on the best technologies to use. We take a strong position on the importance of exploring the institutional and social consequences of proposed means for implementing technologies.

At the January, 1980 San Francisco meeting of the AAAS an all day symposium was held to bring together persons concerned primarily about institutional issues relating the centralization/decentralization issue of energy supply and use. In structuring the symposium, we consciously strove to obtain the best thinking we could find in the area of problems of decentralization. The present volume does not provide an integrated view. What it does is to present concepts. Some are fully developed, while others are at early stages. Taken together the papers illustrate new ways of apprehending social issues relating to energy.

The focus is on institutional issues. There is little discussion of technical feasibility, reliability, systems integration, or comparative economics. No doubt, these issues are crucial. Yet the feasibility and perceived economics of many energy systems is crucially dependent on the institutional matrix in which they are embedded. Often decisions are shifted by these perceptions, and attitudes thus take on an importance which can transcend engineering. At issue is the fundamental question of "what is it that one is trying to accomplish." Traditionally, in the energy sector, this has generally been to provide a specific type of energy (electricity, fuel for space heat) at the lowest possible cost. As the energy debate mounts, the decision criteria go far beyond this simple idea. Centralization/decentralization debates emphasize the position that energy choices are intimately related to social values and freedom of choice.

This should come as no surprise. The OPEC oil embargo of 1973 and the attendant energy price increases have led to a transfer of wealth to OPEC which is the largest wealth transfer in the history of the world, making the flow of gold during the Spanish occupation of the Americas seem small in comparison.

The papers in this volume are organized approximately as follows: the policy framework (papers by Levine and Craig; Holdren; Hyman and Hores); institutional experiences (Gerlach); action programs (Ferrey); and the larger, international picture (Lonnroth, et. al.). We summarize the perspectives of the papers very briefly in this introduction, but encourage the reader to read the full papers in those areas of special interest.

The first paper, by Levine and Craig, challenges the "rationalist view" of energy decision making. According to the rationalist view, man acts as an economic optimizer and selects his investments so as to obtain the best return. This view is shown to fail dramatically when applied to investment in energy conservation in buildings. Throughout the U.S., investment in minimization of energy use is far less than it ought to be based on economic criteria. This was the case even before the energy price increases associated with the embargo of 1973, and it continues today in the face of high energy prices. The paper demonstrates that it is even more striking today. The paper argues that it is a proper role of the government to introduce policies which move in a direction that will encourage people (local decision makers) to move their decisions toward those that correspond to economic optimal investments. According to this view, "barriers" to energy conservation are attitudes or institutions that prevent or discourage investments which are economically optimal. The vantage point of the paper is incomplete in that it does not address the impact of uncertainty on decision making, or of the risks of a failure of an investment in a new and unproven technology. Nevertheless, the overall case is compelling. Man frequently does not act "rationally", and a policy which assumes that he does is doomed to failure.

John Holdren, writing about the environmental dimension of energy decentralization, argues that environmental issues are no longer peripheral to energy decision making, but are rapidly becoming the key factors determining which technologies will prove socially acceptable. The nub of the matter is the rapidly growing recognition that "externality costs" can be large. These externalities include direct pollution effects, but also include the costs of uncertainty associated with large systems that may be put out of action by accident or other events. The paper offers no answers, but presents a typology for systematically thinking about environmental externalities in a period of rapidly growing complexity of energy systems. The line of reasoning suggests that there may be many situations where decentralized technologies are substantially cheaper to the society than centralized ones, especially when the full set of social costs is taken into account.

Barry Hyman and Cliff Hores provide a valuable overview of the approaches that have been taken in four recent studies of the role of decentralized energy systems. The studies included national, regional, and local cases. One of the most important issues addressed by the authors is the question of whether the methodologies used in the studies are transferable to other evaluations of decentralized energy systems. Such transferability could be limited because of the local and specific nature of the resources, the differing institutions in different locations, and a multiplicity of local factors that might not be amenable to generalized analyses. However, from their scrutiny of the four different energy decentralization studies, the authors conclude that the methodologies are transferable and that future systematic studies of decentralized energy systems will profit greatly from the approaches taken and the data gathered and analyzed in the studies to date. The authors see this conclusion as a basis for an expectation of increasing sophistication in the understanding of the relationships among institutional issues and energy decentralization.

Luther Gerlach is primarily interested in evidence regarding the debate about "hard" and "soft" energy futures that can be gleaned from two sources: recent controversies over "hard" and "soft" projects in the United States at the present, and anthropological information from throughout the world on conflict resolution and cultural change. While a stark dichotomy between "hard" and "soft" paths can be made on paper, Gerlach argues that the real processes of conflict and decision in our society produce mixed tactics, strategies and objectives. Often groups opposing a centralized project will appeal to centralized government to achieve a desired end. Many groups and individuals who opposed one type of centralized project, for example, nuclear power, will favor another, such as mass transit. The approaches taken in establishing a controversy and eventually resolving it do not appear to involve pure local or decentralized actions and actors against their centralized counterparts, but mixtures of forces on all sides.

Gerlach addresses the question: can society tolerate the disharmony caused by combining rather than opposing centralized and decentralized projects, programs, strategies and objectives within the energy field? His conclusion is that the conflict between approaches to energy is not nearly so great as the apparent conflict within many cultures over matters of direct bearing to everyday life. Inconsistencies within cultures are routine. Gerlach presents one case of a primitive society shuttling between two cultures and living comfortably with the mores of both. People are pragmatic, and will use whatever tools are available to achieve their desired ends.

Gerlach's conclusion is that energy is not likely to lead to irreconcilable choices between decentralized and centralized energy futures. Rather, both futures appear capable of coexisting, although not without conflict and disharmony among them. But the conflict appears to be one consistent with the resiliencies of society.

Ferrey addresses a wide range of policy and institutional issues affecting the commercialization of renewable energy systems. His paper is suggestive of action programs while recognizing clearly the inherent conflicts among diverse social and energy related goals. He presents an interesting and complex perspective of an analyst who is deeply concerned about the plight of urban America, is supportive of renewable energy, and perceives the real world difficulties of implementing solar energy systems. The paper uses a great deal of data to illustrate such issues as possible biases against the poor and against renters of policies to promote renewable energy; physical limitations of solar energy in urban areas; inequities of property taxes with respect to solar; and numerous other complex interactions among renewable energy systems, urban areas, electric utilities, and existing and evolving institutions. Ferrey sees these facets of the economic and social environment as elements of a mosaic that can be built in harmony with decentralized energy systems. But one has the sense that this harmony will not be attained early.

In "Sweden Beyond Oil", Lonroth, et al examine two complementary futures for Sweden, one based predominantly on nuclear power, the other on solar energy. The same end use demands are required in both cases, and there is an assumption that all Swedes will live as well in 2015 as the top 10% live today. The paper argues that both a nuclear and a solar future are technically possible, but that institutional differences are vast. There is a consensus in Sweden that the best near term strategy is to keep long term options open. Accordingly, the paper concentrates most of its attention on identifying approaches that will allow Sweden to postpone as many decisions as possible as to which path to follow. Decentralized systems require emphasis on local planning, and will require substantial expansions of authority of local planners. A nuclear future would require substantial increases in central planning and would also require substantial institutional change if most energy is to be provided by nuclear energy in 2015. The primary near term reform needed to maintain maximum flexibility includes: 1) strengthening of local authority, especially in areas relating to district heating and conservation; 2) regulatory reform to assure adequate financing on the local level, and to assure adequate balancing of conservation and supply financing; 3) increased national control over large energy users; 4) state financed procurement and development of new energy technologies, especially smaller scale technologies; 5) national land use planning; 6) electric utility reform to encourage dispersed electric technologies. To maintain choice will require a substantial broadening of the national role in planning, but this is "the price that has to be paid in order to have democratic freedom of choice."

REFERENCES

"Energy Future: Report of the Energy Project at the Harvard Business School," edited by Robert Stobaugh and Daniel Yergin, New York: Random House, 1979.

"Energy: The Next Twenty Years." A Report Sponsored by the Ford Foundation and Administered by Resources for the Future, Hans Landsberg (Study Group Chairman), Cambridge: Ballinger, 1979.

"Energy in America's Future: The Choices before Us," A Study by the Staff of the RFF National Energy Strategies Project, Sam Schurr (Project Director), Baltimore: Johns Hopkins University Press, 1979.

Joskow, Paul W., "America's Many Energy Futures - A Review of Energy Future, Energy: The Next Twenty Years, and Energy in America's Future." Bell Economic Journal, 11, #1, 377-398 (1980).

Dubos, René, "The Despairing Optimist." Scholar 49, #2, 151:156 (1980).

Part 1

The Policy Framework

Mark D. Levine, Paul P. Craig

1. Energy Conservation and Energy Decentralization: Issues and Prospects

AN EXTRATERRESTRIAL ENERGY SPY

A friend of ours recently spotted an unidentified flying object. As the UFO departed, our friend found a document that was inadvertently left behind. It was apparently an evaluation of the energy problems of the earth, prepared by someone from an advanced civilization. We share with you the executive summary of the report because we find it to be of great interest:

> The evaluation of the policies and problems of energy on earth was a difficult and confusing assignment. I decided first to focus my attention on one country, the United States. The United States, though a declining economic power at this time, still produces and consumes more energy, of all different types, than any other nation of the world.
>
> My findings were so confusing to me that I decided to input the data base into our most powerful computer, JNYX. JNYX studied the data for some time. Its first readout was rather startling: "AFTER TEN HOURS OF ANALYSIS, I AM UNABLE TO UNDERSTAND THE INFORMATION. THE DATA ARE INCONSISTENT AND NOT SUBJECT TO RATIONAL ANALYSIS. PLEASE INSTRUCT." Never before had JYNX spent so much time with so little results.
>
> However, JYNX did agree to review this report and has done so. With its help, I have drawn the following conclusions from my brief study:
>
> First, there is a very strong belief--especially in the United States--in economics as a means of allocating scarce resources such as energy. Thus, persons and nations with money are able to use as much energy as

they wish while those with little money must be very frugal. Although this causes great problems for many nations and people, there is a widespread belief that the economic system is the most efficient way of distributing scarce resources. I can understand the logic of this idea, but I am greatly confused about the way that the economic principles are applied. For example, most authorities in the U.S. Department of Energy believe that the least costly energy technologies that work well should be used.

However, these same people support projects like synthetic fuel conversion and processing facilities that are extremely expensive. Furthermore, in their private lives they pay more than a dollar per gallon for gasoline when they could pay 30 cents per gallon to purchase a more efficient automobile.* An investment in energy conservation for a new house in Washington, D.C. is equivalent to paying 22 cents per therm of gas (versus gas cost of 34 cents per therm) and 1.5 cents per kWh electricity (versus 4.4 cents per kWh). Similarly, the Nation invests $2 billion to build a new power plant when it could have invested $1 billion in more efficient air conditioners and other equipment and used the remaining $1 billion for other purposes. To make this situation even more confusing, the same people who advocate using the economic system to obtain energy from the cheapest sources are also most in favor of $2 billion power plants. I cannot imagine an official of the Intergalactic Federation who would long survive advocating the waste of $1 billion on a purchase of a $2 billion piece of equipment. <u>This extraordinary conflict between a belief in economic rationality and behavior inconsistent with economic rationality is, I think, a root cause of major energy problems.</u> But it leaves me fully perplexed.

Second, there is considerable debate about the abundance of energy resources and how long they are likely to last. I scanned the literature and discovered that the estimates of resource availability varied by

*An average car is driven 10,000 miles per year. A rough estimate for the cost of improving the efficiency of an automobile from 20 to 30 miles per gallon is five hundred dollars. The reduced expenditure for gasoline over the life of a car (about 100,000 miles) is thus $1670, made possible by an extra investment of $500. This is the equivalent of paying 30 cents per gallon of gasoline not used!

greater than a factor of 25. At the lower end of this estimate, the earth (and particularly the industrialized nations) will suffer terrible economic consequences within a decade. They are doing little about finding alternate energy sources, so I conclude that their leaders are not particularly worried about the scarcity of economic energy resources. There does exist a fringe group that speaks of the "limits of growth" and there are people who speak of "soft paths" and decentralized renewable energy systems and energy conservation. These people make some interesting points, but they do not exert very much influence in high government circles.

Third, I have been baffled by the oil situation in the United States and other countries. The United States acts curiously when it is threatened. Recently, many of its citizens were prepared to go to war because 50 of its people were captured by students in a far away country. And yet, when the United States is really threatened, as they are by the price increases and uncertain availability of world oil (controlled by an international oil cartel), they do very little. I have mentioned that an attempt is being made to produce liquid synthetic fuels from coal at very high costs. Yet there are large quantities of garbage distributed throughout the country that people pay money to remove and dump, when it could be converted into scarce liquid fuels at a cost much lower than converting coal to liquid energy forms. But the garbage is dumped and the coal is mined.

Many U.S. experts have predicted that there will be a severe oil shortage in less than ten years. These same experts have shown that a shortage of oil will cost the United States billions of dollars, will cause severe unemployment and have disastrous effects on the world economy. And some of the experts have shown ways that half of the oil imports could be conserved over the next ten years, at a cost of less than 60 cents per gallon of gasoline. What is the response? Mainly synthetic fuels at $2.00 per gallon or more, with little chance that they can be ready in significant supply short of twenty or thirty years. Even so, the problems associated with liquid fuels are apparently very serious. I do not understand why these people and their leaders are willing to court economic disaster and social upheaval when they apparently value their economic goods, material possessions, and social institutions so much.

> I could go on and on with the contradictions that I have found in the energy policies of the United States. But I think at this point you can agree with me that there is no rational basis for the energy policy actions of the leading world power. I remain most perplexed by the belief in economic rationality combined with the irrational behavior of the people in their energy decisions and policy. Please inform if you wish continuation of the investigation.

DISCUSSION OF ENERGY ISSUES

The report from our extragalactic visitor has raised many important issues. They have several common themes: as oil resources are declining and severe shortages (caused by an inability of world productive capacity to keep pace with growing demand) are expected within the decade, the United States continues to waste energy in large quantities. Extreme anomalies are present in our energy system and in the processes by which decisions are made about energy: we spend vast sums of money to expand energy supply, when there are much better investments that can be made to increase the efficiency of energy use. We are, in effect, wasting our most valuable resources (time, labor, materials, and energy) in providing goods and services to our economy. This is, as our visitor has stated, an irrational way for us to proceed. We wish first to understand why this has come about in order to propose policy remedies for the problem.

Energy Decentralization, Values, Lifestyle, and Behavior

These issues lead directly to the theme of energy decentralization. Indeed, we believe that the theme of energy decentralization is in many ways a unifying concept that will clarify many of the difficulties that our observer had in understanding the U.S. energy system. Devices that <u>use</u> energy are distributed throughout the society; they are totally decentralized. They are not nearly as efficient as they could be or ought to be, given the high value of energy. Decisions about energy-using equipment are not and, in our society, cannot be made centrally. They result from a vast array of individual choices made by every person and every organization in our economy. Thus, though the Department of Energy official who is designing a synthetic fuels program may be seen from one perspective as producing plans that are inconsistent with the efficient production, allocation, and use of energy resources, it is his role as energy <u>user</u> that most forcefully points up the conflicts within our energy decision making process. He shares this role as an energy user with everyone else in the nation and, if he is typical, he is probably more irrational in his personal decisions about energy than he is in his professional decisions.

Decentralization from this perspective begins with technology as a means of improving our efficiency as we go about our business. But it is intimately related to institutions, for the innumerable decisions on energy using systems are made at every level--by individuals, by businesses and industry, by banks and other lending institutions, and by governments. The primary challenge of implementing decentralization is that of changing the criteria by which the array of energy decisions are made.

The term decentralization has often been used to imply lifestyle changes. This is, in our judgment, a correct interpretation of the implications of energy decentralization. As the recognition of the scarcity and high value of energy spreads through society, people will learn to adapt their lives to changing circumstances. An example of one possible adaptation has to do with the American love affair with the automobile. Not too many years ago, a giant Cadillac was the ultimate symbol of success. The prestigious nature of this possession was enhanced if the owner replaced it every year with a new, and probably larger, model. No doubt these values continue in many parts of the country. But GM, our most profitable auto manufacturer, has recognized that a luxury car that appeals to the status seeking qualities of many Americans (especially American males) can be built smaller, be made reasonably efficient in its use of gasoline, and still provide its most important end product: status. And, incidentally, it can provide transportation as well. In time, owning a super efficient automobile could come to confer status on its owner; indeed, in many circles, the possession of a large, wasteful automobile is regarded as a display of poor judgment rather than success. As the critical threat of oil import cutoffs grows, the possession of a gasoline wasting automobile may generally be seen as unpatriotic and a social incentive to purchase efficient cars may emerge.

In this paper we are concerned with the present and the immediate future; we do not expect lifestyle and value changes to play a large and immediate role in changing our energy use characteristics. However, as the stresses on the energy system grow, as the inconveniences of over-consumption of energy (e.g., long lines for gasoline) are increasingly suffered, as our ability to conduct foreign policy becomes restricted (already clearly recognized in our dealings on the Middle East), and as uncertainty in energy price and availability increasingly interferes with countless business decisions, changes in values and lifestyles will of necessity take place. It is not a question of if these changes will occur; it is rather a question of when they will take place and if they will occur in time to avoid an otherwise extremely painful set of events. It is preferable that the adaptations occur in time to avoid great suffering and misery, especially since those least equipped to deal with economic adversity (generally the poor) are likely to bear the brunt of the suffering. But we know little about the time constants associated with basic changes in attitudes and behaviors related to our use of energy.

We do, however, have considerable information about the technical and economic factors associated with improving the efficiency of energy use. We also have some knowledge about the decision making process that has directed our patterns of energy use. We now attempt to put this information to use in an attempt to explain the phenomena that our extragalactic visitor found so "confusing" and so unyielding of "rational explanation".

Understanding the "Irrationality" of the Consumer's Energy Decision Making

One explanation for the seeming irrationality of our energy decisions was the low price of energy and its ample availability over the past decades. With very low energy prices, the consumer had little incentive to invest the time and effort to obtain information in order to improve his decisions. Furthermore, even though we are now suddenly faced with rapid increases in energy prices, it takes time for people to change their habits and devote attention to learning about ways to reduce energy needs or obtain energy appropriate sources.

This explanation, while providing some answers to our dilemma, is not the entire story. We reach this conclusion by investigating behavior in the early 1970's, before energy prices began their precipitous rise. Back in 1970, a kilowatt hour of electricity cost about 75 percent as much as today (in constant dollars) and natural gas cost about 60 percent as much as today. At those prices, it would have made good economic sense for a new gas-heated house in Washington, D.C. to have R-38 ceiling insulation, R-19 wall insulation, and double glazing, and substantially more insulation if the house was heated by electricity (Levine, *et. al.*, 1979). Instead, in 1970 an average house in Washington, D.C. had less than R-9 insulation in the ceiling, practically no insulation in the walls, and single glazing. Thus, back in 1970 the average new home purchaser chose not to make investments in energy conservation that would have save $50 (1970 dollars) per year on fuel bills at a cost of less than $25 per year. We need to look beyond the low historical energy prices for a full explanation of the economically irrational under-investment in increased energy use efficiency.

The relatively low total annual fuel bill (rather than the low per unit cost of energy) that prevailed for many years provides a second explanation for the behavior of consumers. In 1972-1973, total annual expenditure on gas and electricity was about $340 (in 1972 dollars) per household or about 3.5 percent of annual income for a middle class person. Perhaps $100 per year could have been saved by investing in simple and straightforward energy conservation measures in the home. This was apparently an insufficient savings to motivate the investment of time, labor, and money in energy conservation for a middle class home owner. For nation's poor during the early 1970's, the annual household energy bill is estimated to have been $280 (Newman and Wachtel, 1975). Although a smaller expenditure than that of wealthier households, the energy bill amounted to more than 10 percent of income for the lowest income groups. The lower income groups might therefore be expected to take the trouble to save $50 or $100 per year. However, there are two reasons why they did not do so: (1) most of the poor people do not own their own homes; they are therefore unlikely to invest in home improvements unless they are committed to remain in the same place for many years. There is little incentive for the property owner to invest in energy conservation, because it is invisible and cannot easily justify an increase in rent. (2) For the low income families that own their own homes, the availability of capital is so limited and the cost so high that they are precluded from making significant investments in energy conservation, even if the investment is paid back in one or two years. In short, the annual savings have historically either been so small (for the middle economic classes and above) or so difficult to achieve because of borrowing limits (lower economic classes) that very little investment has been made in energy conservation.

Recent studies have shown another facet of this situation: the investment criteria used by consumers in their purchase of energy using equipment (furnaces, air conditioners, refrigerators, and houses) are notably different from the criteria used to invest income in, say, real estate or the stock market. In particular, consumers have typically required a return on investment of 40 to 100 percent in their purchase of equipment to improve energy end use efficiency (Hausman, 1979; Levine, et. al., 1980). The two explanations offered above-- low historical energy prices and total fuel bills-- may partly account for these results. A third factor, lack of information about cost effective energy conservation measures and a failure to understand that sound investment criteria should be applied to purchases of energy using equipment, has certainly played a role in the decisions of tens of millions of consumers; they have passed up excellent opportunities to invest in energy conservation in favor of less desirable investments in other areas.

A fourth factor also plays a major role, particularly in explaining why very large improvements in energy end use efficiency are rarely purchased. This is the general unavailability of products of very high energy efficiency in the marketplace. Examples of the impossibility or difficulty of purchasing very energy efficient equipment abound. Refrigerators that use less than 40 percent of the energy of an average refrigerator, at an increase in first cost of 5 percent or less (and with a return on investment of 80 to 100 percent per year) can be produced with current technology (ADL, 1977). However, no manufacturer in this country is currently marketing such a refrigerator. Automobiles that obtain about 45 miles per gallon are now commercially available (the Volkswagen Rabbit Diesel), but 95 percent of all cars sold in the United States obtain about half of this gasoline end use efficiency. (Here, at an extra cost of $1000 for a very efficient diesel engine, the effective cost of gasoline not purchased because of the energy conservation investment is 60 cents per gallon.) New houses could be tightly caulked to reduce heat loss through air infiltration and equipped with a mechanical ventilation system (fan and ducts) and a heat recuperator to recover heat. Such a house would use less than 60 percent of the energy used for space heating in a typical house. The energy conservation investment would be equivalent to paying 75 cents for each dollar of natural gas not used.

These examples all have one thing in common: the energy efficient equipment which produces these large energy and dollar savings is not widely available in the market place. Thus, if a consumer wishes to purchase an extremely efficient refrigerator or house, he can only do so at enormous inconvenience to himself.

What is the cause of this deficiency in consumer products in a land that has greatest variety of products (more than 100 brands of toothpaste!) known to man? We don't know the full answer, but it is some combination of limited interest in energy conservation as a marketable commodity by manufacturers, wholesalers, retailers, and advertisers and little demand for energy conservation in consumer products by the purchasing public. While it is true that energy conservation has played a role in recent advertising, the claims of "energy efficiency" in most products (e.g., automobiles) are ludicrous when compared with the technical and economic opportunities for achieving high energy efficiency levels.

Understanding the "Irrationality" of the Energy Industry's Decision Making

The discussion thus far has addressed only part of the issue raised by our extragalactic visitor who was baffled by the lack of economic rationality exhibited by the Americans who ostensibly believed in the economic efficiency of the marketplace. It attempts to account for the under-investment in energy conservation by the final consumer of products. But it does not explain why the energy industry is so eager to invest in large, centralized energy supply technologies when cheaper means are available to accomplish the same ends. We believe that this phenomenon is one of the fundamental but little recognized causes of our energy problems.

The decision maker on the new power plant costing $2 billion is the electric utility (and its regulators). This decision maker has choices to make among many different technologies but he considers only technologies that produce electricity. Although the electric utility's product is electricity, electricity is not what the consumer really wishes to purchase. The end user wants services such as refrigeration, air conditioning, and lighting which can be obtained through the use of electricity. If another energy source were available to produce the same end services at half the cost and no added inconvenience, the consumer would surely be satisfied to convert to the use of this new fuel. Thus, the electric utility is primarily concerned with the cost and convenience (i.e., reliability, availability) of producing and distributing electricity; the consumer is primarily concerned with the cost and convenience of final services (refrigeration, etc.).

The implications of this dichotomy of interests between the electric utility and its customers are significant. The utility planner works on those things over which he has control-- namely supply. Investments in energy conservation are not considered as part of the portfolio of projects that a utility planner evaluates. As a consequence, $2 billion is spent to purchase (but not yet operate) a new power plant when $1 billion would have purchased enough energy conservation to make the power plant unnecessary. And the utility customer, who has insufficient knowledge, incentives, and opportunity to invest in energy conservation, pays for his failure twice: first, in the use of more energy and second, in the use of more expensive energy (because new facilities to generate energy are more costly than the existing ones). The wasted billion dollars on the new power plant is hidden by being spread among all the customers of the electric utility, adding about $25 to the annual bill of a household whose utility serves 2 million customers.* The billion dollar waste occurs and is disguised not because of some nefarious plot to misallocate scarce resources or money by the utility but simply because the total is so widely scattered that no one would think of looking for it. They would not seek it because the waste occurs only in comparison to the costs of a wide variety of decentralized investment alternatives and neither the utility planner nor the regulatory agency evaluates energy supply projects in relation to projects that produce the <u>equivalent</u> services but entail no investment in supply.

As a result of pursuing the centralized rather than the decentralized projects, a billion dollars is wasted (for one new power plant) and until very recently no one even noticed. Further, the additional energy produced detracts from rather than contributes to our lives because no new services are provided, environmental degradation is increased, and resources that could have been used productively are lost.

Summary

We have attempted to explain the curious economic irrationality observed by our visitor as he analyzed the energy situation in the United States. We have identified five factors, each operating in different ways on different decision makers, and at (occasionally) times over the past ten years. These factors are:

---

*A 1000 MW(e) power plant meets the electricity demand of about 200,000 houses. If an electric utility has 10,000 MW(e) of baseload capacity the cost of an additional power plant is spread over about 2 million average customers. If one billion dollars is wasted in building a new power plant instead of investing in energy conservation, and the cost of capital to the utility is 5 percent real (i.e., 15 to 20 percent in current dollars), then an extra cost of $25 per year is borne by each utility customer. Note that in this example the average residential electricity customer would pay an additional $250 per year if he uses electricity from the new power plant and were charged the cost of power from this plant!

1. Low unit price of energy (until mid-seventies).

2. Annual fuel bill a small percentage of disposable income.

3. Lack of consumer information about energy conservation opportunities and lack of knowledge about how to evaluate investments.

4. Unavailability of or very limited availability of energy conserving products in the market place.

5. The inability of energy supply firms to allocate their considerable resources to investments in energy conservation at the end use level.

The fifth factor, unlike the first four, accounts for the enormous investment in large, centralized energy supply projects. The first four factors are important in explaining the failure of decentralized energy projects to achieve anything near their potential during the past decade and before.

We now utilize this information to address energy policy issues confronting the Nation. We attempt to show how a strategy for enhancing the decentralized decision making process on energy can address the issues raised by the visitor and can be based on our understanding of the causes of the economic irrationality of the energy system.

ENERGY POLICY CONSIDERATIONS

Higher Energy Prices and Energy Decentralization

We have noted that higher energy prices alone will not cure our energy problems. We also recognize that they will help begin the cure. The effects of higher energy prices are already visible and are likely to become more visible during the eighties. Several key departures from past behavior of consumers, organizations, and governing bodies can be discerned from a careful assessment of recent developments in energy:

- The projections of energy demand growth have fallen, in many instances precipitously. (See Figures 1 and 2, which show the electricity and gas demand forecasts made for California by the California utilities and the California Energy Commission during sequential years in the 1970's.)

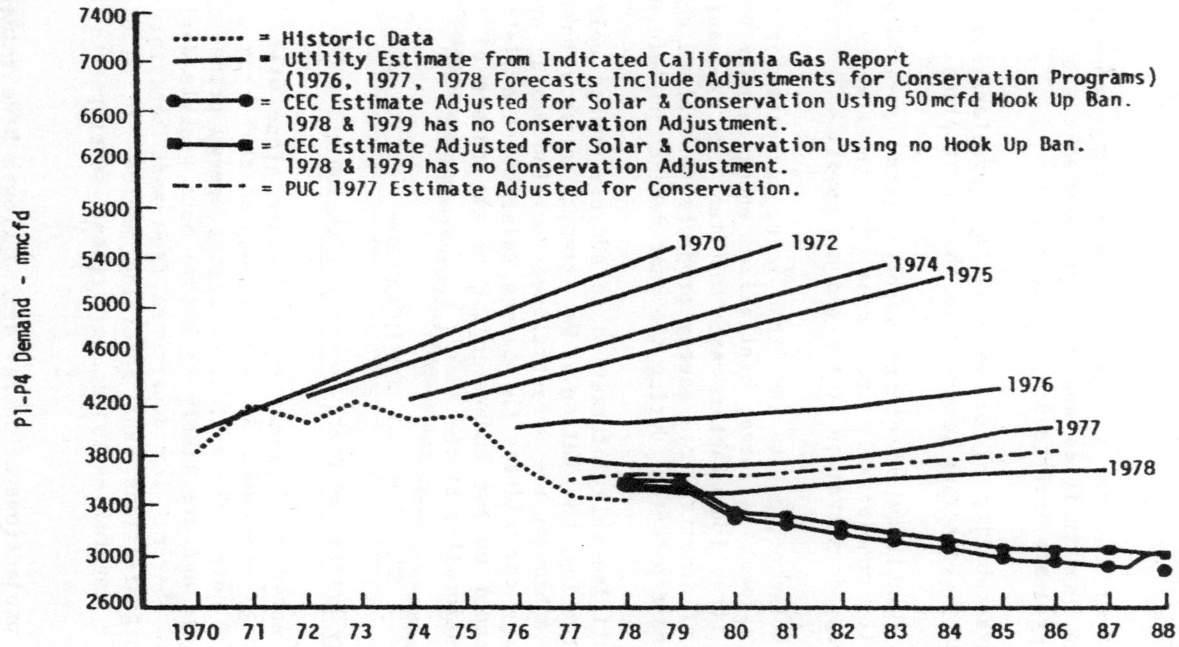

Figure 1. Gas demand projections for California. Utility P1-P4 demand estimate comparison with historic demand, CEC and PUC estimates. P1-P4 demand was determined by using total send out plus curtailment less electric requirement less gas sent to storage. Source: Utility estimates and historic data, California Gas Reports. 1976 electric demand determined from CEC Quarterly Fuels Report using natural gas and fuel oil use. CEC estimates from exhibits in PUC Case No. 10342.

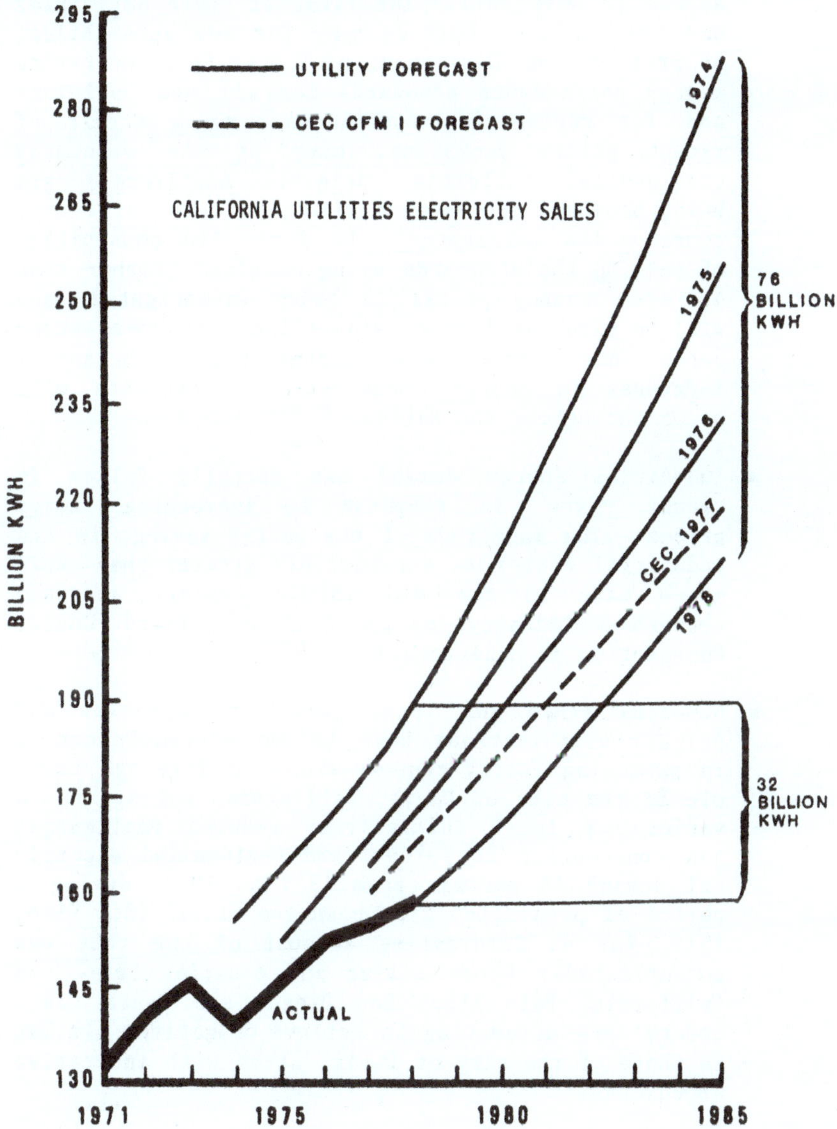

Figure 2. Electricity demand projections for California.

- The federal government has undertaken some major initiatives to bring about energy conservation, particularly in those areas where the market does not appear to work well. The first of these activities was the mandated fuel economy for new automobiles. At present, the Department of Energy is promulgating energy performance standards for all new buildings and for residential appliances. As a result of recent policy decisions, many of the standards (residential buildings, selected appliances) are being proposed at the cost effective level of energy conservation investment! In fact, the possibility of setting the standards using marginal (rather than average) energy prices is being investigated and will be given serious consideration. If these standards are effectively implemented, substantial increases in energy conservation investments will occur throughout the Nation.

- Industrial energy demand has actually fallen in recent years in response to increasing energy prices. The magnitude of the energy savings in the industrial sector is considerably greater than estimates made in the mid 1970's (widely accepted throughout industry) by the Conference Board (Energy Consumption in Manufacturing, 1974).

- Numerous state and local government agencies and private organizations have become extremely active in promoting energy conservation. A foremost example is the city of Davis, California, which, with a variety of local initiatives, reduced residential gas consumption 21 percent and residential electrical demand 13 percent from 1973 to 1977, during a period of population growth in the city. (See Vine, 1979, for an interesting account of how this was accomplished.) Other cities and counties (e.g., in California, Palo Alto, San Diego, and Santa Clara county) are attempting to achieve objectives similar to those of the city of Davis, often with innovative approaches.

- Industrial firms manufacturing and selling energy conservation measures and renewable energy systems have experienced rapid growth. Prominent examples of this growth can be found among manufacturers of home insulation (who were unable to keep up with demand for insulation during 1975 and 1976), heat pumps (a highly efficient way of providing space heat using electricity, with industry experiencing very high growth rates during the past several

> years), solar heaters for swimming pools, and solar domestic water heaters. Other firms manufacturing multiple glazings, heat recovery systems for residential and commercial use, wind energy systems, co-generation facilities, and equipment for the direct burning of organic wastes are certain to see significant growth during the 1980's.

We believe that these activities are just a beginning. They provide a basis for some hope, but they offer little reason for complacency. Energy demand has a curious way of finding new ways to grow and investment in conservation, ways to decline. Nonetheless, there are some reasons to believe that we have begun early and very tentative steps toward energy decentralization.

Higher energy prices relate to energy decentralization by making energy a more visible commodity. In the past, energy was of little interest to most people. Now with a growing recognition that the high price of energy is likely to become even higher in the future, with a widespread concern about the availability of energy supplies, and with a serious international threat to the well-being of the Nation arising from energy imports, almost everyone is thinking about energy. Until now, centralized decision-making has led to centralized "solutions" to the energy problem. These solutions have not worked. Their failure has led to a general acknowledgement of our energy dilemmas. This awareness will, of necessity, lead millions of people to make individual decisions about their use of energy. This, in our view, is a prerequisite for energy decentralization. The challenge is to make certain that these individual decision makers have access to the knowledge and the energy systems that can lead to more rational energy decisions.

The Role of the Federal Government in a Decentralized Energy Future

The federal government is the largest and most centralized organization in the United States. Energy decentralization implies countless decisions by the smallest groups and at the local level. How then do decentralized energy decision makers and a centralized government body coexist under a decentralized energy strategy? Or can they reasonably coexist?

We believe there is no necessary incompatibility between big government and little energy systems. The appropriate scale of a system, whether it is an organization or a technology, depends on numerous technical, economic, and social factors. Our stress on small-scale, decentralized energy systems derives from our sense that they are the best opportunities for our evolving energy system. It also stems from our sense that decentralizing important aspects of our decision-making process puts a large fraction of the responsibility to solve our energy problems where it belongs--on the individual. It does not, however, mean that big is bad, whether the "big" be government or technology. It does mean that we have gone much too far with many of our big systems and have thus missed extraordinary opportunities for making good energy decisions.

The primary role of the federal government is as a means of encouraging decisions that are cost effective when viewed from a societal perspective. It is, in this sense, essential that the federal government provide appropriate incentives for the Nation to make investments in new energy systems that provide a large return on the investment. This return needs to be measured in terms of economic benefits, improvements in the environment, and protection from economic disruption. Such incentives themselves do not differentiate between the scale of technology. However, under the present circumstances in which the decentralized energy solutions have been given little attention and the payoff from their use is so large, appropriate government incentives ought to make clear the advantages of many of the decentralized energy systems. In this view, the government needs particularly to recognize the pervasive barriers to improving energy efficiency and take measures to counteract the forces interfering with rational decision making.*

A second role for the government, in our view, is the more active one of countering the powerful forces that impede our sense of rationality in energy decision making. The government is the only organization with sufficient size and authority to apply corrective measures to the marketplace when it fails to work properly. Thus, the use of energy efficient standards can goad the market into responding as it should, if the standards are set at a cost-effective level of energy efficiency. And the standards, if applied intelligently, can spur a reluctant industry to make efficient

---

*Most of the barriers that interfere with good decision making on energy conservation apply as well to the decentralized uses of renewable energy resources. It is for this reason that we believe that an intensive effort to expand the use of efficient energy using devices will also in the longer term benefit small-scale renewable energy systems. This theme is worthy of considerable analysis, but is beyond the scope of this paper.

products available. However, the standards are likely to be effective only if the population understands that they save both money and energy, as well as reducing critical social problems. Finally, for this understanding to become widespread, an enormous educational process is required.

Big industry is not likely to go away. Unfortunately, most of the political power exerted by the large energy industries is in favor of the large, conventional energy technologies that are, in our judgment, far less desirable than the alternatives to them. (We do not expect the oil companies or the nuclear power industry to suddenly mount a massive lobbying campaign in favor of triple paned windows, R-48 attic insulation, or heat exchangers in houses.) To the extent that political power continues to influence the federal government to provide incentives for the wrong energy systems, we will see the government play a role antithetical to many energy needs of the Nation. To the extent that the government sees itself as playing a role in correcting imbalances in our energy system and recognizes that it can be an agent for positive change, the potential impact of government action in setting a context in which decentralized energy systems can reasonably compete with conventional systems is enormous.

Specific Policy Recommendations

We believe that a number of important policy measures are needed in order to translate the tentative beginnings in the direction of reduced energy use, decentralized energy technologies, and decentralized energy decision making. As stated above, we think that key centralized decisions by the federal government can work in concert with, and indeed encourage, decentralized energy decision making throughout the Nation. We discuss a few of these measures to illustrate the type of policy actions that can overcome or reduce to acceptable levels the energy problems discussed in this paper.

- Energy Efficiency Standards. The energy performance standards for consumer products (appliances, heating and cooling equipment) are important policy initiatives. The fact that some of them (residential buildings, some appliances) are based on economic criteria is highly desirable and has led to much tighter standards than would otherwise have been obtained. These standards are appropriate because of the extensive failures of the market place in these areas, as documented in this paper. However, the approach now taken is just a beginning. There is a need to (1) make the remaining standards (e.g., commercial buildings, certain appliances) consistent with economic criteria, (2) provide strong incentives for industry to produce more efficient products that will meet much stricter standards (while still being economically sound investments), (3) extend the building standards from new buildings to existing buildings, where very large saving in dollars and energy are possible, and (4) ultimately base standards on marginal prices (the true cost of new energy supply), which is possible only when industry has responded to the need for products that are substantially more efficient in their energy use than at present.

- Pricing. We believe that marginal cost pricing, combined with effective and fair taxes on windfall profits, is extremely desirable and will provide a significant boost to many decentralized energy systems. To be fair, the windfall profits tax should apply to all of the increased profits derived from the difference between average and marginal prices. We recognize, however, that marginal cost pricing, even with the difference in revenue between average and marginal prices of energy rebated to the American people, is not likely to be politically acceptable. A second best alternative is to base key energy policy decisions on marginal prices (e.g., conservation standards, incentives for new technologies that compete at the end user level against average prices when new supply competes against marginal prices). The government needs to make people aware of the rapid escalation in energy prices and the expectation of continued price rises. Even more importantly, the government needs to inform people how these prices can rationally influence their decision making on energy. Thus, even without marginal prices, but with a serious educational campaign, many of the effects of marginal prices could be felt.

- New technology. If our case for decentralized energy technologies is accepted, then a new and important role for the government in fostering new technologies emerges. This involves an evaluation of which technologies can pay off (and, as we have suggested, handsomely) in the near term followed by an intensive government role in facilitating their production and sale. We have suggested numerous new technologies that can increase energy efficiency by large amounts at substantial cost savings to the consumer. For some industries, incentives may be useful to help share the risk of a sluggish market. For other industries, standards are needed. Standards with updates stated well in advance can strongly encourage the development of new products that are much more frugal in their use of depletable energy resources than the technologies that are replaced. A strong government role in evaluating and certifying the performance of these new technologies could also greatly promote their acceptance.

- Institution building. No institutional mechanisms for economic tradeoff to be made between investment in energy supply and in increasing energy efficiency. As we have seen, the fact that the electric utility could evaluate only alternative supply options (thus excluding all demand moderating technologies) leads to an enormous squandering of valuable resources. This argues for an extension of the role of traditional energy supply companies into the markets spawned by energy demand technologies. Such an approach clearly requires new institutions or changes in old ones. The most striking example of such changes that are needed are the public utility commissions or public service commissions in each state. These commissions have great influence over all matters dealing with electricity. If their responsibility extended to matters dealing with the services provided by electricity, they could (under the proper framework) more effectively influence energy demand. This is but one example of numerous innovations that are needed to foster a more rational approach to decision making on energy.

CONCLUSION

We have presented our views of the seemingly paradoxical nature and irrationality of the energy system and the decisions that determined its evolution. An economic approach to energy decisions, while widely espoused and generally believed to be the underpinning of our system, does not appear to be functioning in many important areas. The result is an enormous waste of the economic and intangible resources used to produce energy that could be effectively replaced by energy conservation at low costs. This inefficiency in the economic system is, in our judgment, far greater than is recognized either by the public or by "experts". It has led to an over-investment in centralized energy systems and has discouraged the use of decentralized systems that could contribute significantly in the near term to a lessening of our energy problems. There are some signs that the situation is changing, albeit rather slowly. High prices and the widespread recognition of the seriousness of our energy problems have contributed to an increasing involvement of individuals in energy decisions profoundly affecting their future. To achieve an evolution of the energy system in which decentralized technologies (and, in the near term, particularly technologies that improve the efficiency of energy use) play an important role, the government must act forcefully. This action needs to recognize and be responsive to the powerful discriminatory effect of the economic system as it is presently constituted against investments in energy conservation.

REFERENCES

1. California Energy Commission, Biennial Report, 1979.

2. J. Hausman, Individual Discount Rates and the Purchase and Utilization of Energy-Using Durables, Spring 1979, Bell Journal.

3. M. D. Levine and D. B. Goldstein, Chapter 4 and Appendix A in Economic Impacts of Proposed Building Energy Performance Standards, Pacific Northwest Laboratory, October, 1979. (See also BEPS data base, Series VI, to be published in an LBL report by M.D. Levine, et. al., Analysis of Energy Performance Standards for New Residential Houses.)

4. Arthur D. Little, Energy Efficiency of Refrigerators, 1977.

5. D. Newman and D. Wachtel, "The American Energy Consumer," Ballinger Press (Cambridge, Massachusetts), 1975.

6. E. Vine, Planning for an Energy Conserving Society: The Davis Experience,

John P. Holdren

2. Decentralized Renewables: The Environmental Dimension

INTRODUCTION: ENVIRONMENT'S ROLE IN THE ENERGY DILEMMA

Energy for its own sake is not very interesting. We should be interested in energy only in forms, quantities and applications that increase the sum of human well-being. The heart of the energy dilemma--as yet not widely recognized as such--is that the production and use of energy exert negative influences on well-being no less fundamental and pervasive than the positive ones. That is, while supplying energy to the economy contributes to the production of a stream of economic goods and services generally supportive of well-being, energy's disruptions of the social, biological and geophysical components of the environment detract from well-being by diminishing the stream of environmental (nonmarket) goods and services these components provide. It follows from the scaling of the economic and environmental links to well-being as energy use increases (diminishing marginal returns on the economic side, increasing marginal costs on the environmental side), moreover, that at some level of energy use (and for a given mix of technologies providing it) a further increase in the acquisition and use of energy will produce incremental damages to well-being exceeding the incremental benefits. It is possible, in short, to suffer from having too much energy, too soon, as well as from having (in the more traditional view of the energy problem) too little, too late.

Pondering energy in this symmetric framework suggests a useful way to contrast traditional versus emerging perspectives on what "the energy problem" actually is. Traditionally, analysts have been preoccupied with the economic side of the relation between energy and well-being. It has been presumed that the economic benefits of adding to energy supply invariably outweigh the sum of the economic and environmental costs, and, therefore, the main energy-related threats to well-being have been seen as problems of "too little": depletion, rising prices, and falling security of supply of the particular energy sources--petroleum and natural gas--upon which industrial society has become most heavily dependent. Special attention has also been paid to the high economic costs and long time delays associated with the immediately identifiable alternatives to conventional oil and gas supplies, namely, Arctic and offshore oil, imported liquefied natural gas, expanded coal production, fission reactors, and solar collectors. The complex of issues intertwined in this "too little" perspective includes, among others: the differential impacts of energy shortages on jobs; and uncertainty and dispute concerning the degree to which more efficient end-use of energy can be elicited by higher prices or by regulation, without undue economic disruption.

Gradually intruding on this traditional perspective has been a growing interest in energy's effects on well-being through environmental linkages. Since the late 1960s, in fact, increased attention to identifying and quantifying environmental costs and to incorporating these into the decision-making process has established the principle that they can be important enough to justify postponement, significant modification, or even abandonment of specific energy-supply projects. Environmental costs of energy supply that have come under intensified scrutiny in this period include, among others: loss of life and health from pollution and accidents; disruption of climate, nutrient cycling, and other environmental processes; contribution of nuclear power to the rate and extent of proliferation of nuclear weapons; social impacts of precipitous regional development in support of energy facilities; and effects of energy choices on such sociopolitical variables as civil liberties, the role of technical elites, and the degree of centralization in decision making. These increasingly pervasive concerns suggest that what the political trauma over short-term energy choices reflects is not an inability to expand energy supply at some cost but rather a growing perception that the cost--when economics and environment are considered together--is too high. This phenomenon of increased attention to the environmental side of the energy/well-being relation--and, accordingly, to the "too much" interpretation of where energy related threats reside--is not a temporary aberration. It is the initial phase of a natural transition to a perspective on the energy problem shaped as much by awareness of environmental constraints as by fascination with narrow economic measures of well-being. This broader perspective recognizes that the balancing of costs and benefits through <u>all</u> the links between energy and well-being determines how much energy should be provided and, more fundamentally, how much energy-derived good can be done. It follows that environmental characteristics of energy technologies, including especially the scale and rates of change of social and environmental costs at high use rates or high cumulative usage, must become central rather than peripheral factors in choosing one mix of sources over another.

ENVIRONMENTAL ASSESSMENT: THE STATE OF THE ART

Adopting the perspective just described places an enormous burden on the capacity of environmental and social science to assess actual and potential damages and on the capacity of institutions to embody the results in policy. I give most attention in this section to the environmental science (narrowly construed) part of this problem.

The present capability to assess systematically the environmental effects of alternative energy options falls far short of what is required. Appreciation of the complexity of the problem and of the limited progress made on it to date may be facilitated by considering the sequence of tasks that would make up a complete assessment, as follows[1,2]:

1) identification of the sources of effects on the environment, in the form of specific energy systems and activities (Table 1);

2) identification and characterization of the insults to the immediate environment that are produced by these sources, where "insult" is taken to encompass what is put into, taken out of, or otherwise done to the surroundings (Table 2);

3) analysis of the pathways by which these insults lead to stresses on the components of the environment at risk (Table 2);

4) characterization and quantification of these stresses (Table 2);

5) analysis of the consequences for human well-being, which consist of or result from the responses of the components of the environment at risk to the stresses imposed (Table 3);

6) assessment of the associated costs, these being quantitative (although not always monetary) measures of the consequences (Table 4).

Table 1. Sources of Environmental Effects

Energy Supply Options	
PHOTOVOLTAICS	COAL
	Central electricity
SOLAR HEAT	Small fluid bed
Passive	Gasification
Active space and water	Liquefaction
Industrial process	
	NATURAL GAS
SOLAR COOL	Domestic
Passive	Imported
Active	
	OIL
SOLAR THERMAL ELECTRIC	Domestic
	Imported
WIND TURBINES	
On-site	OIL SHALE
Central	
	NUCLEAR LWR
HYDRO	
Existing large dams	INCREASED END-USE EFFICIENCY
New small dams	
	OTHER NON-FUEL OPTIONS
BIOMASS	On-site storage
Waste	Central storage
Selective harvesting	Industrial cogeneration
Energy farms	District heating
Steps Within an Option	
Exploration/evaluation	Storage*
Harvesting	Conversion
Processing/refining*	Marketing
Transportation/distribution*	End-use
Phases Within a Step	
Research	Dismantling
Development/demonstration	Management of long-lived wastes
Commercial construction	Environmental controls**
Operation and maintenance	Regulation and monitoring**

* May occur more than once.

** Occurs simultaneously with other phases but may have its own effects.

Table 2. Insults, Pathways, Stresses

Insults

Use of Resources: Land, water, energy, non-fuel materials

Material Effluents: Solid, liquid, gaseous, including radioactive materials

Electromagnetic Radiation: Ionizing, microwave, other

Noise

Heat

Other Physical Transformations: Blast, modification of surface or underwater topography, vegetation removal, erection and operation of structures and machinery

Sociopolitical Influences: Altered employment opportunities, altered investment opportunities, altered vulnerabilities, weapons temptations

Pathways

Media: Air, water, ice, soil/rock

Processes:	Diffusion	Evaporation	Transport by organism
	Conduction	Rainout	
	Convection	Suspension	
	Radiation	Fallout	

Stresses

Reduced resource availability

Altered chemical concentrations in air, water, soil

Altered circulation patterns in atmosphere, water bodies, ground water

Altered temperature, humidity

Altered electromagnetic fields

Absorbed radiation dose

Perceived noise

Other alterations to or loss of habitat

Sociopolitical stresses

Table 3. Consequences of Responses to Environmental Stresses

Consequences
Deaths from Accidents and Sabotage
Occupational; public
Direct Production of Illness and Disability
Occupational; public; somatic; genetic
Economic Goods and Services Lost or Foregone
Direct damage to crops (e.g., by air pollution)
Direct damage to property
Goods and services foregone because resources needed to produce them were used to produce energy instead
Damage to recreation and tourism
Damage to Environmental Goods and Services
Damage to agriculture and forestry due to climate change, disruption of nutrient cycles, loss of natural pest controls, soil loss, disruption of environmental water storage and flow regulation
Damage to ocean fish and shellfish production (e.g., by oil spills and destruction of estuaries)
Disruption of natural controls on agents and vectors of human disease
Accumulation of toxins by undermining environmental purification processes
Damage to other protective environmental processes (e.g., ozone shield)
Loss of genetic information (hence opportunities for new drugs, crops, and so forth)
Aesthetic Loss and Nuisance
Impaired visibility, ugly structures, annoying noises and odors, diminution of environmental diversity
Psychological Distress
E.g., among persons displaced by energy technology, or fearful of other costs whether or not they materialize
Undesirable Social and Political Change
E.g., increased centralization of political power, loss of civil liberties
War
E.g., over access to energy, or pursued with energy-related technology

While the literature of environmental science and environmental economics is replete with analyses that attempt to trace a given insult from a given source all the way through this sequence to quantitative estimates of consequences and costs, the major assessments and assessment tools that attempt to deal with a variety of energy technologies on comparable footing are reasonably comprehensive only in their treatment of the first two tasks--identification and characterization of sources and insults.[3]

The most important such tools in widespread use are MERES--Matrix of Environmental Residuals for Energy Systems--which is part of the Energy Model Data Base at the Brookhaven National Laboratory, and SEAS--Strategic Environmental Assessment System-- developed at the Environmental Protection Agency and now in use at the Department of Energy.[4] The most recent major attempt at a comprehensive assessment of energy alternatives using these tools and other available information is the work of the Risk/Impact Panel of the National Academy of Sciences' Committee on Nuclear and Alternative Energy Systems.[5]

A major attempt to extend an analysis based on SEAS in order to obtain regionally disaggregated measures of at least some consequences and costs of some insults has been recently completed at the Solar Energy Research Institute.[6]

It should be clear that the measures of insults to which the major comparative assessments largely confine themselves--tons of sulfur oxides and curies of radioactivity released, acres of land disrupted or occupied, acre-feet of water consumed, and so on--are but poor proxies for measures of actual consequences to human well-being.

Much of the effort devoted to date to examining the consequences of energy's environmental effects has focused on direct damage to human health by accidents and effluents, with substantial intellectual and financial resources having been dedicated to identifying kinds of effects, quantifying the damages in terms of increased morbidity and mortality, and converting these damages into dollar costs for inclusion in planners' balance sheets.[7] Damage to property and loss of recreational opportunities also have lent themselves to substantial attempts at quantification and expression in monetary terms.[8] "Indirect" damages to human well-being in the form of diminished environmental services--functions such as climate regulation, water management, nutrient cycling, control of pests and disease organisms, and detoxification of wastes-- have received much less attention. The reason for this is the difficulty in identifying precisely the services

Table 4. Costs and Other Criteria for Evaluating Severity

Costs and Related Criteria
Magnitudes of Responses
Expected deaths, days of life lost, dollar "values" of same
Expected cases of disease, days of activity lost, dollar values of same
Dollar value of resources used (measures intensity of competing demands)
Dollar value of economic services lost or foregone
Dollar "value" of lost environmental goods and services (cost of resulting damage to human health or economic goods and services, cost to replace environmental service with technology)
Temporal Distribution of Harm
Instantaneous versus protracted, sooner versus later
Spatial Distribution of Harm
Concentrated versus dispersed
Coincidence of Risks and Benefits
Do the same people pay as benefit?
Scaling
Is the scaling of response to stress linear or nonlinear, with or without threshold?
Resistance to Remedy
Are there easy ways to prevent the damage?

Table 4, continued

<u>Irreversibility</u>

How much time is needed to effect repairs once damage is done?

<u>Quality of Evidence of Harm</u>

Speculation, theory, extensive data
How much uncertainty?

<u>Proxies for Costs</u>

<u>Magnitudes of Insults</u>

Tons of pollutants or material resources, cubic meters of water, square kilometers of land, joules of energy, curies of radioactivity

<u>Magnitudes of Stresses</u>

Ambient concentrations (ug/m^3 in air, ppm in water, g/m^2 on soil)
Secondary Indicators of concentrations (biochemical oxygen demand, pH change)
Concentrations in organisms (ppm, total body burdens)
Rads of absorbed radiation dose
Resource use as a fraction of available flow (renewables) or stock (nonrenewables)
Temperature change
Perturbations in natural processes, as a fraction of natural flows or stocks

---

Table 5. Major Consequences Ranked by Analytic Difficulty and Emphasis to Date

EMPHASIS IN EXISTING ASSESSMENTS AND IMPACT STATEMENTS	INTRINSIC DIFFICULTY OF PREDICTING/QUANTIFYING CONSEQUENCES: LOW	MEDIUM TO HIGH	VERY HIGH
LARGE	occupational deaths & injuries from in-plant accidents, pre-emption of land & water supplies	public deaths & disease from air pollution, water pollution, radioactivity release; occupational deaths & injuries from in-plant toxic substances	public deaths & injuries from large disasters (reactor accidents, dam failures)
MODERATE	public deaths & injuries in small accidents (in, e.g., energy transportation & end use)	impact on recreation opportunities and tourism; property damage by air pollution; fish kills by oil spills, other water pollution, or temperature stress	alteration of regional & global climate by emissions of heat, water vapor, & CO_2; damage to fish & wildlife via habitat disruption
SMALL		redistribution of population & other socioeconomic effects of regional energy development	disease outbreaks due to ecological disruptions; crop damage from pest outbreaks; loss of crop or forest productivity due to altered nutrient cycles

at risk, evaluating the damages to these services, and translating these damages into equivalent monetary costs.[3] These indirect damages may nevertheless represent the most significant category of environmental risks due to energy, where risk is ascribed its formal meaning as the product of the frequency or probability of specified events multiplied by their consequences. Even with respect to the more easily quantified direct effects, moreover, the uncertainties under today's state of knowledge can be very large and the degree of comparability between effects of different technologies (or even different effects of the same technology) is often small. Assessments inevitably must rely to some extent on subjective judgments as to what kinds of risks should be left the greatest margin of safety in the face of these uncertainties and the "apples-and-oranges" problems of comparisons across technologies and effects.

Some aspects of the status of environmental assessment of energy technology are summarized in Table 5, which arranges some of the most important categories of consequences according to the emphasis they have received to date and the difficulty of predicting and/or quantifying them.

ENVIRONMENTAL CHARACTERISTICS OF THE MAIN OPTIONS

If we could assemble and digest the best available information on the environmental effects of the full range of energy options, with all its uncertainties and shortcomings, would we be able to apply our knowledge to the making of policy. My own conclusions, from a necessarily incomplete and imperfect attempt to do this over the past ten years, can be summarized as follows.

No energy option presently known or imagined (not excepting energy conservation, solar energy, or fusion) is without important environmental liabilities. These liabilities vary greatly in severity, however, particularly when one accounts not only for uncorrected impact but also for amenability to amelioration by technical means. Notwithstanding some tendency to prefer those options whose impacts have been least thoroughly investigated, one can conclude with some confidence that the most benign energy option environmentally (as well as the cheapest and fastest) is energy conservation, defined as extracting, more well-being from each unit of energy used. Its liabilities may include the effects on health and ecosystems of producing materials to be substituted for energy (e.g., insulation), toxic effects of choosing and using such materials carelessly (insulation again), contribution of reduced ventilation rates to the hazard of indoor air pollutants, and incremental accident hazard

Table 6. Liabilities of Solid Fossil Fuels and Nuclear Fission, Ranked

---

Fossil Fuels

1. Carbon dioxide and climate
2. Air pollution and public health
3. Acid water and ecosystems
4. Hydrology disruption and water consumption in the west
5. Health and safety of miners
6. Land disruption in surface mining
7. Coal transport accidents
8. Social impacts of boom and bust

* Heavy metals and public health

* Occupational exposures to toxic substances in fuel conversion

Nuclear Fission

1. International proliferation of nuclear weapons
2. Misuse of nuclear weapons by subnational groups
3. Accidents and sabotage at:
   A. Reactors
   B. Reprocessing plants
   C. Spent fuel transportation
   D. Waste repositories
4. Routine emissions and exposures at or from:
   A. Mill tailings
   B. Reprocessing plants
   C. Fuel fabrication plants
   D. Reactors
   E. Uranium mines
   F. Waste repositories

* Centralization of decision-making, reliance on technical elites

* Channeling of world research and development along lines inapplicable to the needs of less developed countries

---

*"Sleepers" which are not yet rankable.

resulting from reduced automobile weight. These are mostly amenable, however, to technical amelioration. The least benign options environmentally are imported oil, the solid fossil fuels (coal and oil shale), and nuclear fission. The most important liability of oil is the actual and potential impact of our heavy use of it on international political affairs (notably our own foreign policy, that of other industrial nations, and the plight of the oil-poor developing countries). The principal liabilities of the solid fossil fuels and of nuclear fission are listed and ranked in Table 6.[9-11] Although much effort and verbiage have been devoted to the comparison of imported oil, coal, and nuclear power, such comparisons are not terribly helpful--they must grapple with enormous uncertainties, many of them substantially irreducible on a time scale of policy interest, and with "apples-and-oranges" problems of the worst kind. Each of these three options entails liabilities of such severity and intractability, moreover, that I find the prospect of a massive expansion in the use of <u>any</u> of them appalling.

Between the "best" and the "worst" options environmentally are the renewables (notably wind, hydropower, biomass, and direct harnessing of sunlight) and fusion. The main generic environmental liabilities of the renewables arise from their land-use requirements (sometimes in fragile or highly prized environments) and from the effects of extracting and processing the materials needed to construct the collection systems. Especially severe specific liabilities are posed by large hydro dams (destruction of rare ecosystems, risk of catastrophic accident, high evaporation losses), irrigated biomass plantations (high water use, off-site effects of fertilizer and pesticide residues), and large windmills if placed in windy locations that also happen to be scenic (coastlines, crests of mountain ranges). The best of the renewables environmentally appear to be building-scale or neighborhood-scale solar heating and cooling systems, direct collection of sunlight for industrial process heat (using focusing collectors or ponds), and fuel production from municipal, agricultural, and timber wastes. A more complete listing of environmental liabilities of renewable energy sources is given in Table 7.[12]

Fusion is many possibilities, not one, the best option probably environmentally falling between the best and the worst renewables, and the worst of them perhaps only marginally better than fission.[13] The main environmental liabilities whose treatment will determine where in this spectrum fusion actually ends up are: a link to fusion weapons (relevant in the inertial-confinement approach to fusion but not in the magnetic-confinement approach); a link to fission

Table 7. Some Possible Environmental and Social Impacts of Alternative Energy Sources.*

ACTIVE/PASSIVE SOLAR HEAT/COOL

	Passive	Active Heat	Active Cool
Construction materials: resource demand, pollutants from their production, accidents in fabrication	x	xx	xx
Accentuation of grid peak in poor weather	x	x	
Relatively high land use to minimize shading	x	x	
Accidents/injuries in rooftop collector maintenance		x	x
Leaks of working fluid: health (?) and property damage		x	x
Leaks of storage medium: property damage		x	x
Removal of shade trees		x	x
Aesthetic intrusion		x	x
Water use for cooling			x

ON-SITE/CENTRAL WIND SYSTEMS

	On-Site	Central
Construction materials and related problems	x	x
Land use for low interference and transmission grid	x	xx
Aesthetic intrusion	x	xx
Accident risk: sudden blade failure	x	x
Bird catching	x	x
TV interference	x	x
Aircraft navigation hazard	x	x
Microclimate effects		x

Table 7, continued

WASTE/FARM BIOMASS SYSTEMS

	Waste	Fuel Farm	Electricity Farm
Impacts of transportation in collection	x		
Land use for collection		xx	xx
Land use for transmission grid			xx
Fertilizer and pesticide effects		xx	xx
Irrigation water		xx	xx
Water use for processing	x	x	
Particles, NO_x, CO, HC from combustion	xx	xx	xx
Explosion in gasifier	x	x	
Occupational exposure to toxic compounds in processing	x	x	
Fire in fuel storage	x	x	x

PHOTOVOLTAIC SYSTEMS

	Dispersed	Centralized
Construction materials and related problems	xx	xx
Toxic effluents from fires	xx	x
Land use and related ecosystem impacts		xx

SMALL/LARGE HYDROELECTRIC DAMS

	Small	Large
Significant evaporation loss of water	xx	xx
Loss of flowing river habitat/recreation	xx	xx
Downstream ecological effects	xx	xx
Potential for catastrophic dam failure	x	xx
Land use/population displacement	x	xx

Table 7, continued

GEOTHERMAL HEAT/ELECTRICITY	Heat	Electricity
Land use for harvesting - subsidence	xx	xx
Land use for transmission grid	x	xx
Water consumption for cooling		xx
Salts - water pollution	xx	xx
H_2S - air pollution	xx	xx
Noise		x

DISPERSED/CENTRALIZED FLUIDIZED-BED COAL BURNERS	Dispersed	Centralized
Mining impacts	xx	xx
Noise and accident risk in coal distribution	xx	x
Water use for cooling	x	xx
Air pollution from combustion	xx	xx
Land use for electricity transmission		xx

*Double x's indicate there is a reasonable probability on present evidence that the problem is serious.

weapons through the use of fusion neutrons to produce fissile material (relevant in both approaches); an inventory of radioactive tritium, likely to be substantial in first-generation fusion reactors (posing a hazard through routine emissions and occupational exposures as well as through accidents); and radioactive materials, some long-lived, produced by the interaction of fusion neutrons with reactor structure (amenable to reduction by clever design and choice of materials).

COUNTABLE EFFECTS VS. EFFECTS THAT COUNT

What such rankings of energy options on environmental grounds do not tell us (and would not, even if the rankings themselves were more generally accepted) is how much a given environmental advantage is worth. Obviously, we should be prepared to pay more in internal (that is, economic) costs for technologies that enable us to pay less in external (that is, environmental and social) costs. The question is: How much more? (The question does not arise if the more environmentally benign technologies also happen to be economically cheaper. This is true of many forms of energy conservation, and Amory Lovins believes it will also prove to be true of the decentralized renewables. I am not as confident of that as he is, and I will assume for the purposes of this discussion that there will turn out to be a number of important cases in which more benign options are costlier economically than less benign alternatives.) To answer this question seems to require quantifying and monetizing all the important environmental costs of the alternative technologies; yet, as I suggested in the preceding section, the state of art of environmental science and environmental economics is far from adequate to this task. Let me elaborate a bit on this situation and its implications for policy.

Of the galaxy of identifiable effects, only a few have consequences that are readily quantified. Among those that are quantifiable in principle, many are still characterized by huge uncertainties; one can write down a number (for example, for the annual excess deaths produced by the air pollutants from a coal-burning power plant of specified characteristics in a specified location), but it is probably wrong by a substantial margin. (This has been called the tyranny of illusory precision.) And among consequences that can be quantified with reasonable accuracy, few can be unarguably monetized; conventions exist, for example, about the value of a human life and of a day of labor lost, but their existence does not mean they are satisfactory. Costs that cannot be monetized, of course, cannot be readily compared, or at least would not be compared in the same way by people with different values, preferences, or tastes. (This is the apples and oranges problem again.) I would argue, further, that the environmental costs of energy are likely to prove that the most important effects are precisely those most resistant to quantification and monetization: for example, the proliferation of nuclear weapons, carbon dioxide and climate, the destabilizing politics of oil, the plummeting prospects of the poor countries because energy choices in the rich countries (who in an important sense choose for everyone) are irrelevant to poor-country needs.

The intractability of this situation is compounded by the frequent separation of costs and benefits in space and time; that is, different people are receiving the economic benefits than are paying the environmental costs. The fossil fuels and the nuclear option are particularly pernicious in this respect, because so many of their insults produce consequences of global and intertemporal reach. (Think of carbon dioxide, heavy metals, mutagens, and precursors of acid rain from fossil fuels, proliferation, nuclear terrorism, and long-lived radionuclides from nuclear power.) Substantial parts of the burdens these insults produce will be borne by populations far removed in space and time from the consumption and the decision on how to supply it--future generations, the populations of poor countries most susceptible to climate-induced famine, or, in other cases that come to mind, specific populations of energy-industry workers exposed to pernicious occupational hazards and of Indians whose ancestral lands happen to be underlain by coal. And the fact that most of these burdens are unquantifiable or nonmonetizable means that the beneficiaries could not compensate the victims even if there existed the will and the institutional machinery to effect the transfer. This separation of benefits and costs is deplorable for two reasons. First, it is unfair. Second, it is inefficient, because it prevents signals, essential to rational decision-making about energy, from registering with those making the decisions. In other words, the only way for consumers of energy to know how much is enough is if they experience the full costs--economic and environmental--of their consumption. Geographic and temporal separation of costs and benefits prevents this, and the resistant nonquantifiability and nonmonetizability of many of the most important costs precludes rectification of the problem through the market. The result will be certain overconsumption and probable disaster.

THE CASE FOR DECENTRALIZED RENEWABLES

Attempts to minimize the foregoing difficulties must rely on a combination of the following four approaches:

(1) Choose technologies whose intrinsic characteristics keep the magnitude of external costs small compared to internal ones.

(2) Devise management strategies that shift costs from the external to the internal category.

(3) Devise management strategies to distribute resistant externalities (those that cannot be internalized) in a pattern that coincides with the technology's benefits.

(4) Choose technologies amenable to approaches (2) and (3) over those with resistant externalities that by their nature are exported in space and time.

A great deal more attention need be paid to the search for the best specific measures with which to pursue these approaches, but past and ongoing investigations into the environmental characteristics of unconventional energy technologies suggest a line of argument that I believe will assume increasing importance in the energy debate over the next decade.

The essential point is that the environmental costs of many of the unconventional (mainly renewable) energy options, while certainly not zero, are (i) smaller in magnitude than those of most conventional options, (ii) often easier to internalize than those of the conventional options, and (iii) even where resistant to formal internalization, tend to be borne mainly by the users of the energy and in proportion to their use.

For example, consider the class of environmental consequences of renewables--occupational injuries and illnesses in materials acquisition and facility construction and operation--that has received more attention than any other and is widely held to represent their biggest environmental liability.[14-16] Significantly, this particular class of environmental costs is not only amenable to drastic reduction (occupational injuries and illnesses in many of the relevant industries are unnecessarily frequent and could be reduced at modest cost), but resistant hazards exceeding the average risk of all occupations can be reflected in differential wage rates (higher pay for more dangerous jobs), which at least partly internalizes this environmental cost into the price of the energy.[17-18]

Many of the other environmental consequences of renewables, while not so readily internalized, are borne mainly by the users of the energy because of the decentralized character of the technology--energy capture, conversion, and end-use taking place in close proximity. Aesthetic nuisance from rooftop solar collectors and small windmills, damage or toxic effects from leaking or burning collectors, and accident risk and television interference from small windmills all fall in this category.

Some environmental effects of renewables, such as air pollution and water pollution during the processes of material acquisition and component fabrication, do take place far from the point of energy use and have the potential for far-reaching consequences qualitatively similar to some of those of burning fossil fuels. Studies of this problem have shown, however, that it is quantitatively much smaller than that produced by getting the same amount of energy from fossil fuels.[19-20]

Of course, some renewable energy technologies are environmentally much less attractive than others. Centralized forms of solar or wind electricity generation--for example, large solar-thermal-electric or photovoltaic installations in the deserts or arrays of giant windmills lining seacoasts and mountain crests--would share the tendency of conventional energy sources to export their environmental costs away from the energy users. In terms of damage to ecosystems, hydropower is perhaps more destructive per unit of energy output than any other energy technology, renewable <u>or</u> nonrenewable.[19] Biomass combines some of the environmental liabilities of conventional fuels (e.g., air pollution upon combustion, although it contains less acid-producing sulfur per unit of energy than coal or oil and it makes no net contribution to the carbon dioxide problem) with those of large-scale, intensive agriculture (e.g., off-site effects of fertilizers and pesticides). The more decentralized approach to biomass utilization--harnessing wastes from existing agricultural and forestry operation, plus municipal wastes--avoids these latter liabilities.

If the alternatives to be used are chosen carefully from the large menu of renewable energy options, then, emphasizing the decentralized varieties, it seems likely that society can fashion an energy system that is not only physically sustainable but relatively equitable--in the sense that the largest environmental costs are not exported in space and time but rather are borne by those who choose the technologies and use the energy. This crucial set of advantages, and not their arguable economic edge over other energy options,21 may turn out to be the most persuasive rationale for the vigorous development and implementation of the decentralized renewables.

REFERENCES

1) Budnitz, R.J., and Holdren, J.P., 1976. "Social and Environmental Costs of Energy Systems." Annual Review of Energy 1: 553-580.

2) Holdren, J.P., 1978. "Environmental Impacts of Energy Production and Use: A Framework for Information and Analysis." In Energy Information, William W. Hogan, ed., Institute for Energy Studies, Stanford University.

3) Holdren, J.P., Harte, J., and Tonnessen, K., 1979. "Environmental Data Bases and Integrated Models as Assessment Tools: A Critical Survey of Accomplishments, Potential, and Limitations." In Proc. Workshop on Integrated Assessment for Energy-Related Environmental Standards, Office of Technology Impacts, U.S. Department of Energy, Washington, D.C.

4) House, Peter, 1977. Trading Off Environment, Economics, and Energy: A Case Study of EPA's Strategic Environmental Assessment System. D. C. Heath and Co., Lexington, MA.

5) Risk/Impact Panel of the Committee on Nuclear and Alternative Energy Systems, 1979. Risk of Energy Systems. National Academy of Sciences, Washington, D.C.

6) Yokell, M.D., Lawrence, K.A., and Shaheen, Jr., A., 1979. Environmental Benefits and Costs of Solar Energy. Report SERI/TR-52-074, Solar Energy Research Institute, Golden CO., September (DRAFT).

7) Lave, L.B., and Seskin, E.P., 1977. Air Pollution and Human Health. Johns Hopkins Press for Resources for the Future, Baltimore, MD.

8) Fisher, A.C., and Peterson, F.M., 1976. "The Environment in Economics: A Survey." Journal of Economic Literature 14: 1-33 (March).

9) Holdren, J.P., 1978. "Coal in Context: Its Role in the National Energy Future." Houston Law Review 15: 1089-1109 (July).

10) Holdren, J.P., 1977. "U.S. Electricity Through the Year 2000: Coal or Nuclear? Some Issues in Resources and Environment." In CRC Forum on U.S. Electricity Through the Year 2000, Budnitz, R., ed., CRC Publishing Co., Cleveland, OH.

11) Nuclear Energy Policy Study Group, 1977. Nuclear Power Issues and Choices. Ballinger Publishers, Cambridge, MA.

12) Holdren, J.P., 1978. "Environmental Impacts of Alternative Energy Technologies for California." In Distributed Energy Systems in California's Future, P. Craig et. al., eds., Lawrence Berkeley Laboratory Report LBL:6831-Revised, Vol. II, March.

13) Holdren, J.P., 1978. "Fusion Energy in Context: It's Fitness for the Long Term." Science 200: 168-180 (14 April).

14) Caputo, R., 1977. An Initial Comparative Assessment of Orbital and Terrestrial Central Power Systems. Jet Propulsion Laboratory Report 900-780, California Institute of Technology, Pasadena, March.

15) Inhaber, H., 1979. "Risk with Energy from Conventional and Non-conventional Sources." Science 203: 718-723 (23 February).

16) Holdren, J.P., Anderson, K., Gleick, P., Mintzer, I., Morris, G., and Smith, K.R., 1979. Risk of Renewable Energy Sources: A Critique of the Inhaber Report. Report ERG 79-3, Energy and Resources Group, University of California, Berkeley (June).

17) Thaler, R., and Rosen, S., 1975. "The Value of Saving a Life: Evidence From the Labor Market." In Household Production and consumption, N. Terleckyj, ed., Bureau of Economic Research, New York, NY.

18) Yagi, N., and Fisher, A.C., 1979. Cross-Cutting Issues in Integrated Environmental Assessment of energy Alternatives: The Cost of Occupational Hazards. Draft Report to the Office of Technology Impacts, U.S. Department of Energy, Energy and Resources Group, University of California, Berkeley (October).

19) Harte, J. and Jassby, A., 1978. "Energy Technologies and Natural Environments: The Search for Compatibility." Annual Review of Energy 3: 101-146.

20) Davidson, M., and Grether, D., 1977. The Central Receiver Power Plant: An Environmental, Ecological, and Socioeconomic Analysis. Report LBL-6329, Lawrence Berkeley Laboratory, University of California.

21) Lovins, A.B., 1978. "Soft Energy Technologies." Annual Review of Energy 3: 477-517.

Barry Hyman, Clifton Hores

3. Comparative Analysis of Decentralized Energy Studies

INTRODUCTION

A major alternative to the continuation of post World War II energy usage and supply patterns is the "soft path" approach which has been promoted by Amory Lovins and others. A major feature of these soft energy technologies and systems is decentralized energy generation.[2] Furthermore, and as a consequence of this decentralization, the increasing interest by community, municipal, state and regional groups in exploring the possibility of a soft energy path for explicitly defined geographic areas raises several interesting questions regarding analytical studies of their feasibility. Such studies, conducted for specific purposes in specific areas, should be expeced to be site specific. However, while unique local conditions will obviously affect the manner in which each study is carried out, there might be certain features of the analyses which are broadly applicable. If so, information on lessons learned and techniques adopted by one group can benefit subsequent studies. This would be particularly beneficial because the state-of-the-art of conducting decentralized energy analyses is relatively primitive.

This paper compares the approaches taken in several recently completed studies of decentralized energy. Included in the comparison are studies of on-site solar energy by the Congressional Office of Technology Assessment (OTA),[3,4] a distributed energy system for California,[5,6] decentralized electricity generation in Washington State,[7] and a renewable energy strategy for Franklin County, Massachusetts.[8]

These four studies were selected because they are well documented and represent a spectrum of approaches to the subject. One of these studies (OTA) has a national perspective, two of them are focused at the state level, and one is county-oriented. Three corners of the country are represented (northeast, northwest, and southwest), each with their own unique geographical and economic characteristics. Also, participants in each of the four studies were present at a recent symposium on regional soft energy paths and had the opportunity to exchange information about their respective projects.[9]

The first part of this paper consists of a brief review of each study's purpose, geographic scope, funding, staffing and duration. This review establishes a context for evaluating each study's methodologies and may be useful for those groups contemplating alternative structural arrangements for pending decentralized energy studies. The second, and major, part of this paper examines the methodologies used to address five major areas of substantive inquiry: definition of decentralized energy systems, selection of technologies appropriate for such systems, techniques employed to match supply and demand; methods for estimating the costs; and procedures for examining the impacts of implementing such systems. Specific findings, recommendations and accomplishments of each study are of secondary interest in this paper since we do not expect the results to be as generalizable as the methodologies employed. The methodological section of the paper is followed by a brief review of the current status of implementation of each study. Our conclusions draw upon the lessons learned from the four studies and suggest promising techniques for utilization in future efforts.

OVERVIEW OF STUDIES

OTA Study

The specific purpose of this study was to review the potential of on-site solar energy systems as alternatives to continued reliance on centralized energy generation and transmission systems. The geographic scope of the study included the entire United States, although data for various on-site systems were tested and compared against conventional energy supply systems in four cities selected to represent the range of climates and fuel prices found in this country.

An OTA staff team organized and synthesized the work of a variety of contributors. Several consultants and contractors produced material for the final report; additional support was given by the OTA Solar Advisory Panel and Energy Advisory Committee, as well as a number of other individuals. Approximately $600,000 was invested in the project over a two-year period. The final report was published in June 1978 and was the first of the four studies reviewed in this paper to be completed.

California Study

The California study attempts to examine the feasibility of relying on local renewable energy resources through a decentralized, or distributed system. The study provides a state-wide focus while allowing for regional and local variations in energy patterns. California exemplifies the advanced post-industrial economy toward which the country is moving, and thus may provide valuable lessons for the rest of the nation.

The study was initiated in 1977 as an effort to analyze the assertions made for the environmentally benign character of the soft path.[10] It was conducted as a joint project of the University of California at Berkeley and Davis, Lawrence Berkeley Laboratory, and Lawrence Livermore Laboratory.

The project was funded by a $200,000 contract from DOE in June, 1977, virtually all of the work was completed by that September, and a two-volume interim report was published in March, 1978. Due to the study's time limitations, no citizen advisory apparatus was utilized.

Franklin County Study

The purpose of this study was to compare the continuation of a traditional energy generation and distribution system which currently serves Franklin County against a renewable energy future emphasizing a decentralized energy system.

A major goal of the project was to ". . . educate the public and local decision makers about a malleable energy future, and allow them to chart their own futures."[11] To attain this goal, an ambitious citizen involvement strategy was undertaken. Throughout the study, the cooperation between county citizens and project staff contributed to the final product. In this respect, the Franklin County study differs from the OTA, California, and Washington studies which had little or no involvement by the general public.

The project was conducted at the Future Studies Program at the University of Massachusetts, Amherst. DOE provided $30,000 to fund the development of the alternative scenarios. The project team went much further than originally contemplated, adding the environmental impact analyses, economic summary, and implementation sections to the expected report.

The Franklin County project began in the fall of 1977, and was published in April, 1979. Both the OTA report and the California interim report were completed within this period, and while the Franklin County report made several explicit references to the California project, no citation was made of the OTA study.

Washington Study

The study on decentralized electricity generation for Washington examines alternatives to current plans for supplementing the existing regional hydroelectric system with large coal and nuclear power plants. The Washington study differs in scope in three major ways from the other studies discussed in this paper. First, it is the only one which examines nonrenewable as well as renewable energy resources as part of a decentralized system. Second, it is confined to decentralized electricity generation, whereas each of the other three considers electricity as well as non-electric energy forms. Third, the state-wide analysis is coupled with site-specific case studies designed to focus on particular applications of a specific technology.

The project was carried out by the University of Washington's Program in Social Management of Technology and staff members of the House and Senate Energy and Utilities Committees of the Washington State Legislature. An advisory committee met bi-monthly to guide the progress of the project.

Funding came from a Ford Foundation grant supplemented with matching funds from the State Legislature. Total resources for the study amounted to approximately $200,000. Initiated in January of 1978, the final report was published in December 1980. As the most recently completed study of the four reviewed in this paper, the Washington project has benefited substantially from the others and the documents published by the other studies were utilized extensively in this project.

COMPARISON OF METHODOLOGIES

Definitions of Decentralized Energy

Adopting a working definition of "decentralized energy" is by no means a trivial task; on the contrary, there is no commonly agreed upon terminology. We begin with Lovins' definition of "soft" energy as technologies which rely on renewable energy flows; are diverse, making many individually modest contributions to our national energy supply; are flexible and relatively low technology; are matched in scale and geographic distribution to end use needs; and are matched in energy quality to end-use needs.[12]

Other investigators have adopted certain elements from Lovins and utilized them in connection with different terminology. In doing so, some investigators have either ignored certain aspects of the concept of "soft," or added additional elements to suit their own needs. In particular, each of the four studies discussed in this paper relies on a different key word to describe the focus of its investigation. For OTA, the key word is "on-site"; the California study uses the term "distributed"; Franklin County employs "renewable" as the primary descriptor; and "decentralized" is the term utilized in the Washington study. A further variation on the terminology is seen in the use of "decentralized renewable" in the title of the symposium for which this paper was prepared. This diversity is significant, especially since two of the above-mentioned studies (California and Franklin County) were explicitly inspired by Lovins' earlier work. Even when common terminology is used, the working definitions can be quite different. For example, at a recent workshop at the Solar Energy Research Institute, eleven different definitions of "distributed" energy systems were proposed and discussed.[13] This lack of a clear definition can inhibit productive research and be a source of misunderstandings between different researchers.[14]

The OTA project adopted a scope of effort which was restricted to examining "on-site direct solar" energy systems. Although the OTA report frequently refers to the analysis contained therein in terms of a comparison with a "centralized" system, the restriction to "on-site direct solar" technologies certainly means that OTA looked at only a narrow range of alternatives to centralization. Thus, the project was not confronted with the task of dealing with a much wider variety of possible energy systems over which a single working definition had to be cast.

In contrast, the Washington study dealt with the problem of defining decentralized energy by considering degrees of decentralization associated with many technological and organizational variables. The list of variables included facility size, siting flexibility, nature of the basic energy resource, degree of grid independence, facility ownership, financing mechanisms, and extent of government regulation. The Washington study also distinguishes between a decentralized energy facility and a decentralized <u>system</u> of energy facilities. According to this approach, a given facility or system is likely to be more decentralized with respect to some variables than others, and while it might be easy to compare any two facilities or systems with respect to a single <u>aspect</u> of decentralization, it is difficult to make such a comparison in terms of a generalized concept of decentralization. An even more difficult (and perhaps not very productive) exercise is the effort to generalize about the decentralized character of generic technologies.

One of the California project managers explained that the "diversity of their project staff thwarted any consensus on a definition."[15] The closest the California study comes to a working definition is the distinction it makes between the basic energy resource and the energy conversion technologies. With regard to the former, a distributed energy system is defined as one that is based on "indigenous, sustainable" resources.[16] In this respect, the California approach is consistent with that used by Lovins. However, when it comes to the conversion technologies in a distributed energy system, the California study goes no further than describing these technologies as "decentralized, or distributed."[17]

The Franklin County effort draws directly from Lovins' writings but narrowly interprets Lovins' soft path as "a system of energy supply...that utilize(s) renewable, nonpolluting sources of energy production."[18] But the report goes beyond Lovins in recognizing that the various attributes of these energy sources may be either advantageous or disadvantageous, "depending on the value system of the individual."[19] We elaborate on this notion of "desirability" of technologies in the following section.

Selection of Technologies

Both the OTA and Franklin County projects examined technologies which a priori satisfied their definitions of decentralized energy. There were no attempts to select the most promising of these technologies from a wider range of available technologies through utilization of a systematic selection process. The "on-site direct" solar energy technologies included in the OTA project were solar passive and active space and water heating, photovoltaics, and high temperature solar thermal (with and without co-generation). Franklin County examined direct solar heating, solar co-generation, photovoltaics, wind, hydro, wood, and other forms of biomass.

Although Franklin County explicitly invoked Lovins' definition of "soft" technologies as the basis for choosing its technologies, it did not evaluate the extent to which the selected technologies met this definition. In fact, it is apparent that the only criterion actually employed was that of a renewable energy resource, incorrectly inferring thereby that all technologies based on renewable energy resources are automatically "soft."[20]

Seven of the California criteria for evaluating candidate technologies were based on Lovins' description of "soft" technologies; an additional criterion was that the technology had to be "close to engineering feasibility today, and have the potential of becoming economically competitive by the end of the century."[21] A decision analysis type model was developed in which each of eight candidate technologies could be rated with respect to each of these criteria to arrive at a ranking of the relative desirability of the candidate technologies.[22] However, neither that model nor a separate ranking of 22 technologies with respect to 11 environmental impact categories were used in a systematic manner to select the technologies for inclusion in the study. While giving a skeletal rationale for the rejection of several technologies, no explicit analysis is provided as leading to the selection of the following five: hydro, geothermal, solar for space and water heating and industrial processes, biomass and wind.

A much more elaborate version of the decision analysis model sketched out in the California study was used by Washington to select the five "most desirable" technologies from a list of twelve. Forty-six "desirability" characteristics were identified and grouped into eight categories: potential contribution, technical performance, economics, resource availability, safety, environmental impact, siting opportunities, and socio-political performance. The relative desirability of each of the 12 candidate technologies was established with respect to each of the 46 characteristics. This led to small hydro, total energy systems, photovoltaics, cogeneration and wind being selected.

Note that in contrast to both the Franklin County and California studies, the Washington analysis distinguishes between the characteristics of a "decentralized facility (or system)" and the characteristics of a "desirable technology." While some of the 46 "desirability" characteristics identified by Washington are related to either the Washington definition of "decentralized" or to Lovins' definition of "soft", many of them were arrived at independently of such concepts.

Matching Supply and Demand

OTA examined the performance of prototypical on-site solar systems designed to meet the demand of five categories of users. Various combinations of solar as well as conventional components and conservation measures were then studied in applications assumed to be located in Albuquerque, Boston, Fort Worth, and Omaha. No effort was made by OTA to select optimal system design for any of the applications, and performance was calculated only to "establish the credibility of different proposals and to make broad comparisons between competing concepts."[23] There was also no attempt to estimate the overall potential of these systems to meet future energy demand in the sample cities, or in other cities.

The California study specified energy demand levels for California in 2025[24] and constructed hypothetical supply systems to meet the projected energy requirements. Detailed end-use demand estimates were based on calculations made by the National Academy of Sciences Committee on Nuclear and Alternative Energy Systems (CONAES),[25] modified as necessary to fit the needs of the California study.

The four scenarios for California consisted of the combinations of a centralized/distributed energy system in which demand is based on energy prices doubling/quadrupling. The two distributed supply scenarios matched end-use with the distributed energy supply technologies selected earlier. For the centralized case, the technologies utilized to meet energy demand were hydroelectricity, geothermal (both of which were used in the distributed case also), nuclear and coal power plants, and synthetic natural gas and synthetic liquid fuels (both derived either from coal or oil shale). In both the centralized and distributed cases, it was assumed that oil and natural gas were used only for feedstocks.

In matching supply technologies to various end uses in the distributed scenario, the California study assumed that all residential and commercial space and water heating requirements would be met by direct solar heat, and that all industrial process heat below 350°F and 40% of industrial process heat above 350°F could be provided via on-site solar co-generation units. The supply/demand matching exercise revealed that even assuming 100% collectability of all state-wide biomass residues and conversion of these residues to methanol, a substantial shortfall occurs in the ability to provide liquid fuels for transportation purposes. Because of this projected imbalance, two additional scenarios were run in which all urban transportation was assumed to occur in electric vehicles. Even with this modification, the projected demand for liquid fuels was greater than could be provided by methanol derived from indigenous sources of biomass. The resulting shortfall in liquid fuels is "the major technical problem"[26] in the distributed energy scenario.

The Franklin County study examined several supply/demand projections for the year 2000. Four "traditional path" demand models originally developed for providing national projections were adapted for use in Franklin County. These ranged from a low growth model with an annual demand increase of 1.4% to a case with an annual consumption increase of 3.9%. The project also developed a demand projection for the "soft path" scenario including county-specific end-use estimates for electricity, space and water heating, direct process heat, and liquid fuels for industry and transportation. These demands were calculated by using current energy usage patterns in Franklin County as a starting point, assuming widespread adoption of conservation measures and accounting for certain trends in the commercial, industrial, and transportation sectors. The resulting Franklin County "soft path" scenario involves a <u>reduction</u> in end-use energy demand between 1975 and 2000.[27]

The approach used by Franklin County in estimating end-use demand for its soft path scenario is very similar to the methodology used in the California study, with two important exceptions. First, the California study made more consistent use of the CONAES results, applying them across all sectors, whereas Franklin County used the CONAES results only in estimating appliance energy requirements. Second, California used the same demand estimates for both centralized and distributed cases while Franklin County used its own county-specific end-use forecast for its soft path scenario, but relied on adaptations of national demand estimates for its traditional path analysis.

The next step in the Franklin County analysis was to match end-use requirements with supply combinations, with most of the supply analysis focused on the soft path scenario. The potential for direct solar energy to meet space, water, and industrial process heating requirements was assessed. A second key part of the Franklin County analysis was a very detailed exercise of matching various combinations of hydro, wind, and wood-fired power plants against the monthly electricity requirements associated with five different demand levels. In addition, an hourly simulation of electricity demand over the entire year (at the lowest of the five annual demand levels) was matched by three supply mixes involving hydro, wind, photovoltaics, and wood before choosing an optimum supply mix.

The demand projection utilized in the Washington project was part of a regional demand forecast maintained and updated by the Bonneyville Power administration. There are three important distinctions between the nature of that demand forecast and those used in Franklin County and California.

First, the Washington study utilized a detailed forecast that had been carried out specifically for the state whereas the others adapted national projections of energy demand. Second, both Franklin County and California involved detailed end-use analyses which assumed adoption of widespread conservation measures. Thus, these studies employed "low-growth" demand forecasts which have credibility among advocates of energy conservation, while the demand forecast used in the Washington study probably has more credibility within the energy "establishment." Third, because of the end-use type analyses carried out by Franklin County and California, their demand projections facilitated matching energy supplies to demands on the bases of the quality of energy required at the point of end-use. In doing so, electricity was reserved for meeting high quality demands, e.g., the Franklin County and California assumed no electricity is used for space or water heating in their respective target years of 2000 and 2025. Considerations of energy quality at point of end-use were not included in the Washington study.

The demand/supply matching employed in the Washington study involved a series of scenarios describing alternative electricity supply systems for the state during the year 2000. The centralized technologies considered were large base-load coal and nuclear plants. A mix of five decentralized technologies for each scenario was sought which, when used in conjunction with the storage capacity of the existing hydrosystem, most closely matched projected monthly variations in electricity demand. The detailed examination of monthly variation in demand for electricity in the Washington study is similar to the process used in the electricity segment of the Franklin County project.

While both Franklin County and Washington assume heavy reliance on hydropower to supply electricity, Franklin County treats all hydroelectric resources as "run-of-the-river" facilities whose energy output is linked to stream flows,[28] whereas Washington makes use of the long term storage capability of existing reservoirs to complement monthly variations in the output of photovoltaic and wind systems. The other major difference in the handling of hydropower potential is that Franklin County analyzed the energy producing potential under typical weather conditions, while the Washington study also examined hydropower capabilities during extended periods of low water conditions.[29]

The outcome of the Washington supply/demand matching exercise indicates that decentralized electricity generation can meet up to half the projected growth in electricity usage between 1980 and 2000 without any serious mis-matches in monthly supply and demand.

Cost Estimates

California was the only one of the four studies that did not carry out detailed cost estimates for the various decentralized technologies. Recognizing the interim nature of their report, the California study team decided to defer a systematic analysis of costs because of the uncertainties associated with such an analysis.

The OTA report provided cost comparisons between several hundred on-site solar technologies and conventional energy systems, based on itemized cost estimates of components and computed for both 1976 and 1985 start-up dates. All comparisons were made through life-cycle costing with the present value of costs based on a 10% discount rate.

As input to the cost calculations, three forecasts for the prices of conventional fuels were used. The base year for the analysis was 1976, and the low forecast assumed that the cost of electricity and fossil fuels would increase at the same rate as inflation, assumed to be 5.5%. The medium forecast anticipated a 41% rise in electricity costs, and a 123% increase in the cost of natural gas by the year 2000 (in 1976 dollars). The high forecast estimated that energy prices would increase by a factor of 3.4 by 2000 (in 1976 dollars). The calculations also investigated the effects of a 20% income tax credit for solar systems and other forms of financial subsidy.

It should be emphasized that the system configurations used in the OTA report are not optimized, so that the costs of professionally designed systems could be substantially below those quoted by OTA. In a similar vein, the electricity supply systems selected in both the Franklin County and Washington studies to meet projected electricity demands in the year 2000 were not selected on the basis of a least cost analysis, but solely on the ability to match monthly variations in demand.

The only life-cycle cost estimates conducted in the Franklin County project were for solar space and water heating; and those estimates are crude in comparison to those used by OTA. However, Franklin County did determine the economically optimum collector areas for several different applications.

The Franklin County solar cost estimates were based on an assumed annual inflation rate of 6% (OTA used 5.5%), with fuel prices escalating at 10% annually. To convert costs to a present value basis a discount rate of 8% was used (10% used by OTA). In addition, Franklin County analyzed the sensitivity of the cost estimates to changes in the basic economic input data. For example, an increase in the discount rate from 8% to 10% reduced the present value of life-cycle savings of an optimized system by 31%; and an increase in the fuel escalation rate from 10% to 12% increased the savings by 63%.

The system cost estimates performed in the Washington study were similar to but not nearly as sophisticated as those done by OTA. The basic economic input data for all cost calculations included an assumed annual inflation rate of 9%, with all fuel prices increasing 11% annually except for uranium which was assumed to be increasing at 12%. Detailed life-cycle costs were calculated for each of 29 combinations of technologies, size, location, and ownership for the decentralized technologies as well as for the coal and nuclear baseload plants. The Washington cost estimates also reflected assumptions regarding deployment rates for new generating plants. Generation, transmission, and distribution costs from each plant were then aggregated to calculate estimated electricity costs in 2000 for each scenario.

Impact Analysis

While each study developed their impact analyses based on the assumption that the decentralized technologies were dispersed throughout the geographical study area, the Washington study also used site-specific case studies as part of their impact assessment. The Washington approach is an extension of that used by OTA, where site-specific case studies were the basis for performance and cost calculations, but not (except as noted below) for the impact analysis. The following discussion will compare the approaches taken in the five major impact areas of economic, environmental, land use, institutional and regulatory, and socio-cultural concerns.

Economic Impacts. The OTA report addressed the employment impacts and the foreign market opportunities of an onsite solar energy industry, but did not systematically examine long term employment impacts.

No in-depth assessment of the impact of decentralized energy futures on jobs, income, and economic development was provided in any of the other three studies. However, the

Franklin County report did propose using an input-output model to carry out such an investigation. Some of the factors which would have to be considered in applying this tool to Franklin County were examined, but the discussion served only to introduce the subject for future study.

Environmental Impacts. OTA examined the air pollutants, waste heat discharges, and solid waste production associated with meeting the energy needs of one of the prototype structures (a single family residence in Omaha) via eight different supply system configurations.[30] They also studied emissions associated with manufacturing various types of onsite solar equipment.

Franklin County undertook a detailed environmental impact assessment for its traditional path by establishing "energy trajectories" for each of the conventional fuels. Environmental attributes were defined along each step in a given trajectory to measure the impacts associated with activities such as mining, transportation, processing, and end-use of a particular energy form. The specific environmental attributes quantified were land and water resources consumed, pollutants emitted, and descriptors of occupational health and safety. These attributes were grouped according to whether their effects were felt inside or outside Franklin County. Summing these impacts over all energy forms contributing to the traditional path resulted in an assessment of the overall environmental impact in the year 2000 for that scenario.[31]

Unfortunately, lack of adequate data prevented the construction of a similar set of energy trajectories for the Franklin County soft path scenario. However, descriptions were provided of the environmental impacts of solar heating, wind, hydro, and a small, wood fired power plant. Of particular interest is the finding that the emissions from a wood fired power plant "will be far less than emissions from home burning of wood."[32] That result demonstrates that a decentralized technology (home burning of wood) does not always pollute less than a more centralized technology (wood fired power plant); and that concepts of "desirability" need to be distinguished from concepts of "decentralization."

The California methodology for environmental analysis requires an identification of the sources of impacts; identifying the inputs to the environment produced by these sources; analyzing the pathways by which the inputs lead to environmental stress; characterizing and quantifying these stresses; analyzing the responses of environmental elements most susceptible to stress; and identifying and quantifying the costs of these responses.[33] This theoretical framework is a valuable contribution of the California study, and is compatible with the energy trajectory concept used in Franklin County. However, in attempting to apply the methodology, the California researchers ran into the same obstacle of inadequate data that their counterparts in Franklin County encountered. As a result, the California environmental assessment was primarily descriptive, rather than analytical. Included was a tabulation of the possible environmental effects and possible serious environmental effects of fifteen distributed technologies.[34]

The Washington project carried out brief descriptive evaluations of the environmental impacts of each of the five decentralized technologies examined as part of that study. However, no effort was made to conduct environmental impact analyses for each of their scenarios. The argument presented for not conducting such an analysis was that unless the location of each facility generation and transmission could be prescribed, a comprehensive quantitative environmental analysis could not be performed. Franklin County and the four cities examined by OTA each represent a much more homogeneous physical environment than either California or Washington, and are therefore more conducive to carrying out a quantitative environmental analysis. The Washington study did, however, perform an environmental assessment for each of its site-specific case studies.

Land-Use. The California study was the only one of the four which comprehensively examined the broad land use implications of decentralized energy systems. Besides examining the land use impacts of specific decentralized technologies (which was also done by the Washington project), the California project systematically studied some major issues in "soft path" land use planning and developed a step-by-step procedure for carrying out such a planning process.[35] The California procedure was endorsed by the Franklin County team[36] as appropriate for local use, but no land use analysis was conducted as part of the Franklin County effort.

Land use issues were covered in each of the site-specific case studies conducted in the Washington study, and important insights were gained as a result. Similarly, the detailed analysis that was carried out by OTA for the OTA prototype installations clarified the land use requirements of specific technologies. A case study of a hypothetical integrated residential-commercial-industrial community with 10,000 inhabitants was performed as part of the California land use analysis. In addition to examining the land use impacts of several configurations of decentralized energy systems to serve this hypothetical community, the prospects for scaling the case study results for application to communities of different sizes was explored.

Institutional and Regulatory. Institutional impacts considered by OTA included a detailed examination of the effect of on-site systems on utility companies, with an emphasis on the technical and economic issues associated with integrating on-site energy generation with the existing electricity generation and distribution system. The OTA report also addressed building codes and solar rights as regulatory issues of on-site solar.

The California report contained an extensive discussion of the different institutional requirements of distributed and centralized energy systems, and paid particular attention to the "managerial/legal control of (energy) production and distribution."[37] This type of analysis is particularly important because issues related to the ownership of energy generating equipment pose some of the most difficult problems in moving toward decentralized energy futures, and there are a wide range of possible owners and contractual approaches to cooperative ownership. Governments, quasi-governmental agencies, utilities, private organizations, and individuals can each own parts of decentralized energy systems and novel ownership patterns may be needed to deal with on-site and community scale systems.

The California report examined the implications of widespread use of these technologies on business opportunities for small firms. Also, a detailed case study of the recently enacted California building code identified the role and attitudes of different interest groups, e.g., lenders, builders, realtors, that will be impacted by adoption of decentralized energy systems.

An analysis is included in the Washington study of capitalization, system management, and operations problems which might be faced by utilities as a result of decentralization of electricity generation. Washington also surveyed potential impacts on licensing agencies and other units of state and local government, unions, lending organizations, educational systems, police departments, and insurance companies.

While several institutional and regulatory issues were briefly identified in the Franklin County project as agenda items for future study,[38] no analysis in this area was performed.

Socio-cultural. An examination of the relationship between energy and the behavior of people was presented in the California study, which identified the following seven dimensions of the "people problem"[39] and examined each of them from a dialectical perspective: conflicts between individuals and organizations; credibility of various participants in the energy debate; intangibility of energy crisis; time perspective of individuals; the role of the expert; attitudes toward regulation; and perceptions of technology as an instrument of progress.

The only other one of the four studies to focus on sociocultural impact was the Washington project. They examined potential demographic implications; changes in political philosophy and balance between interest groups; and notions of independence, safety, and security in addition to several other areas which are included within the California framework.

IMPLEMENTATION OF STUDIES

As the first of the four projects to publish a report, the OTA study has had to endure the most rigorous test of time. Much of that work has been accepted as an authoritative treatment of the direct solar energy alternative.[40] Shortly after completion of the project, Congress held several hearings on the subject;[41] issues raised at these hearings resulted in follow-up papers being prepared by OTA staff ranging from up-to-date economic studies to investigation of small-scale, renewable technologies not covered in the original study.

Like the OTA report, the California study achieved a degree of national recognition[42] even though the published volumes were only intended to be an interim report on the project. However, funding for the project was withdrawn after publication of the interim report, and no final report will be published, at least as originally envisioned. Detailed issue papers on subjects introduced in the interim report are being prepared by former members of the project staff.

The Franklin County project has made the most progress in terms of actual implementation of the study findings. An implementation strategy developed as part of the project has resulted in a three to five year transition period. The project has been moved from the University of Massachusetts to the Franklin County Energy Project and Resource Center. Funded by a six-month, $30,000 DOE grant, this office is managed by the former Franklin County study director. The office has begun implementing the study findings, and has assumed the roles of technical advisor, information clearinghouse, and coordinating center for county energy planning. Further research is being conducted on the economic impacts of a renewable energy future, and the specific applications of renewable technologies in Franklin County. Through community presentations and demonstration projects, active citizen involvement and support has been achieved. Also, Franklin County has formally adopted a set of energy policies emphasizing a shift to renewable energy resources.

The final report of the Washington study has not yet been published; therefore an evaluation of the implementation of the study findings is premature. However, staff members of th House and Senate Committees on Energy and Utilities of the Washington State Legislature have been an integral part of research activities throughout the project. This coordination between the academic researchers and the staffs of the policy makers has been supplemented by approximately a half-dozen briefings over the course of the project to the legislative committees. Prospects of implementation are greatly enhanced by this kind of interaction, and the potential for significant application of the study findings has already been tapped. Recently enacted solar access legislation for Washington was developed and proposed through the channels opened by the decentralized electricity generation project.

CONCLUSIONS

There was significant variation in the approaches taken by the four projects to explore decentralized energy futures. This diversity reflects the inherent ability of decentralized energy systems to match scale and energy quality to end-use needs. Appropriately, the decentralized energy system described in each study was "matched" to the social, economic, environmental, and political needs of the area considered.

Still, the preceding comparison of decentralized energy studies can benefit those considering undertaking similar research efforts. Consideration of funding requirements and sources, team composition, and study duration are useful points of reference for the structural design of future projects. More importantly, the methodologies used to treat the key issues are transferable. That is, in each of those substantive areas examined in this paper, the particular approach used by any one of the four projects could have been used by any one of the other three. Surely the outcomes of applying the same technique in more than one setting would likely be quite different, but there is enormous value in being able to adopt and adapt methodologies from other projects. This opportunity for cross fertilization has already particularly benefited the Washington study, which as the most recent of the four, had access to the published reports of the other three.

If we were asked to assist in the design of a hypothetical upcoming study of decentralized energy in some unspecified community, county, region, or state, we would recommend adoption of the following features of the four studies considered in this paper:

- Following the Washington approach, clear unambiguous definitions of decentralized energy and desirable technologies (not necessarily the same) should be developed and applied in a systematic manner to select the most promising technologies for inclusion in the study.

- Accuracy of any long range demand forecasting is debatable, and selection of a specific demand forecast model is a difficult decision. Development of appropriate data for use in the model is perhaps even more difficult. However, it is important that whatever forecasting approach is adopted should be applicable to the specific geographical area under study. This was done by Washington and Franklin County (for the renewable scenario), while the California study mixed an end-use analysis for California with a model designed for national application. The approach used by Franklin County and California to distinguish between the quality of energy needed for different end uses is an important ingredient of demand estimation.

- When examining the capability of various technologies to meet demand, detailed specification of the individual components and their performance characteristics such as was done by OTA is important. Matching supply to demand over daily as well as annual cycles (as was done by Franklin County) is an important element of system planning, especially for systems relying on weather dependent supply technologies. A common problem that all such studies will have to cope with is the lack of statistically reliable data on the output characteristics of such weather dependent supply technologies.

- A recommended system cost analysis would draw on the following study components: The detailed cost estimation methodology used by OTA; Franklin County's cost optimization and sensitivity analysis; and Washington's effort to aggregate energy costs for individual installations into system-wide costs. When comparing costs of several scenarios, it is important that a consistent methodology and data-set be applied across all alternatives. Analysts should be particularly sensitive to the difficulties of comparing the costs of mature technologies for which ample data are available with the more speculative cost estimates for newly developing technologies whose configurations and performance characteristics are still evolving.

- Examination of the impacts of decentralized energy systems should include economic, environmental, land use, institutional and regulatory, and socio-cultural considerations. The use of site-specific case studies to illuminate impact areas is a valuable tool as was demonstrated by Washington, and by California for its land use and institutional/regulatory studies.

- Any attempt to conduct a broad economic impact analysis of decentralized energy will be hampered by data inadequacies, but the use of an input-output model for the study area, as outlined by Franklin County, is worth considering. This is one area in which a workable methodology is still lacking.

- California's theoretical framework for environmental analysis combined with Franklin County's detailed quantification of impacts and their distribution provide the basis of a strong environmental impact section. The California approach to examining land use issues adds an important dimension to such an analysis.

- OTA's treatment of the general impact of decentralization on utility companies, Washington's focus on potential financing difficulties, and California's examination of the private sector each raise important institutional issues for further examination.

- In the socio-cultural area, the groundwork laid by the California and Washington studies provides a useful start for future analyses.

If a hypothetical study of a decentralized energy system were to include all of the features outlined above, it would probably remain hypothetical due to lack of funding and staff resources to carry out all of the analysis. However, to the extent that some of the above elements can be adopted with little change from the earlier studies, those tasks will be made easier. As each new study improves upon the earlier work in selected areas, the methodologies will become increasingly sophisticated.

The development of an information dissemination and communications network among active researchers in this field will be a necessary step to realize this transferability of methodologies. As more decentralized energy studies are carried out, they will be able to benefit from the work of their predecessors. A storehouse of knowledge will be accumulated and better techniques and procedures will result.

REFERENCES

1. Lovins, Amory B., and Hugh Nash. The Energy Controversy. San Francisco: Friends of the Earth, 1979, p. 23.

2. Lovins, Amory B. Soft Energy Paths: Toward a Durable Peace. Harper Colophon, 1977, p. 40-41.

3. Application of Solar Technology to Today's Energy Needs, Volume I, Office of Technology Assessment, U.S. Government Printing Office, Stock No. 052-003-00539-5, June 1978.

4. Application of Solar Technology to Today's Energy Needs, Volume II, Office of Technology Assessment, U.S. Government Printing Office, Stock No. 052-003-00608-1, September 1978.

5. Distributed Energy Systems in California's Future, Interim Report, Volume I, U.S. Department of Energy, HCP/P 7405-01, March 1978.

6. Distributed Energy Systems in California's Future, Interim Report, Volume II, U.S. Department of Energy, HCP/P 7405-01, March 1978.

7. Decentralized Electricity Generation for Washington State, Final Report, Program in Social Management of Technology, University of Washington, December, 1980.

8. Franklin County Energy Study: A Renewable Energy Future, Future Studies Program, University of Massachusetts, April, 1979.

9. Dartmouth/SERI Symposium on the Design of Regional Soft Energy Paths, Report DSD #127, Resource Policy Center,

Thayer School of Engineering, Dartmouth College, September 12-13, 1978.

10. Ref. 6, Cover letter.

11. Ref. 8, p. 10.

12. Ref. 2, pp. 38-39.

13. *Decentralized Energy Studies*, Progress Report No. 2, Solar Energy Research Institute, SERI/PR-53-220, April, 1979, pp. 6-10.

14. See Ref. 1 for many claims by Lovins that his concept of "soft" has been misinterpreted.

15. Private conversation with Mark Christensen.

16. Ref. 5, p. iv.

17. Ibid.

18. Ref. 8, p. 5-6.

19. Ibid.

20. Ibid., pp. 134-135.

21. Ref. 5, p. 10.

22. Ref. 6, pp. 265-276.

23. Ref. 3, p. 31.

24. The year 2025 was selected as the earliest year by which a complete turnover of the state's capital could be achieved. Such a turnover was considered to be an important prerequisite toward achievement of a distributed energy supply system.

25. "U.S. Energy Demands: Some Low Energy Futures," *Science*, Vol. 200, April 14, 1978, pp. 142-152.

26. Ref. 5, p. vii.

27. See Ref. 8, pp. 152, 159, 175, 181.

28. A storage capacity of 10-12 hours is used to help meet daily peak demands.

29. All Pacific Northwest electricity supply planning is

based on the need to supply electricity during an extended period of low water conditions.

30. Ref. 3, p. 224.

31. See Ref. 8, pp. 518-519, for a summary table of environmental impacts.

32. Ref. 8, p. 552

33. Ref. 6, p. 4.

34. Ibid., pp. 18-19.

35. Ibid., pp. 174-175.

36. Ref. 8, p. E-1.

37. Ref. 5, p. 210.

38. Ref. 8, Chapter XII.

39. Ref. 6, p. 183.

40. "Photovoltaic Power Systems: A Tour through the Alternatives," Science, 10 February 1978.

41. Review of OTA Solar Report, U.S. Senate Committee on Energy and Natural Resources, Publication 95-135, June 23, 1978.

42. Luther J. Carter, "A Bright Solar Prospect Seen by CEQ and OTA," Science, Vol 200, No. 4342, 12 May 1978.

Part 2

Institutional Experience

Luther P. Gerlach

4. Dueling the Devil in the Energy Wars

THE DUEL: SOFT VERSUS HARD

Listen and watch people debate how and if we should develop and use key resources of land, water and energy, and it seems that they are really debating not only the desirability, but the viability of two quite different and rival types of futures. If we choose to march towards one, we not only must give up the other, but if we make the wrong choice, we march to economic or ecological catastrophe.

What are the polar possibilities in this dualistic debate? One is envisioned as a future in which expanding economic growth to meet ever increasing demand for high living standards is sought, applying larger scale and more elaborate technology and ever more centralized levels of decision making by ever more comprehensively integrated industrial and governmental organizations to squeeze ever more product from conventional capital resources subject to increasing demand, but found in ever lower concentrations. The rival future is projected as one of growth or economic steady state with more elaborate patterns of redistribution to achieve social justice, applying smaller scale technology and more localized or decentralized decision making and smaller enterprises to develop renewable or recyclable resources.

Following the lead of Amory Lovins, some distinguish between these two approaches to the future as the hard path and the soft path. Advocates of the path called "hard" would reject the implication that hard means especially hurtful to environment or people, but would accept that it means hard science, hard data, and advanced hardware, and as such, is the only rational, viable way to continue on the path of progress which has characterized western society. Advocates of the path called soft would reject any notion that this means soft-headed, using soft science while stressing that it is the path which enables its users to work with nature instead of trying to cut through and conquer it.

The hard-soft debate is perhaps most obviously and dramatically displayed in any sustained protest over coal based or nuclear energy development. The developers argue that the big surface mines, power plants, and the far-flung powerlines and interlocking grids that go with them are necessary to meet the country's vital economic, political, and social needs for a reliable supply of energy. They proclaim their beliefs with advertisements, showing they are investing increasingly, drilling deeper, building bigger, safeguarding more securely, exploring wider with more elaborate technology to provide more jobs and services. For example, energy developers serving a large area of rural and suburban Minnesota were proud of the way they brought together two rural electric cooperative associations (composed of 34 local electrical distribution cooperatives) in a joint venture to build a 1000 megawatt mine-mouth power plant in North Dakota. The plant would convert low quality lignite, surfaced mined using some of the largest draglines in the world, into high quality electricity which then would be brought into the system of regional and local Minnesota grids over a high voltage DC powerline. Initially, they were proud to say this powerline was as large and as advanced as any other DC power line in the country.

Other energy developers in this region were proud of a project which utilized a complex and large scale leverage leasing arrangement to raise considerable construction capital from Wall Street. The project integrated the efforts of a Minnesota-North Dakota rural electric cooperative association (composed of 12 local distribution cooperatives) with a Minnesota investor-owned electric utility to bring power to the iron mining industry of Northeast Minnesota which converts low grade iron ore into high grade taconite pellets for shipment to eastern steel mills. Looking into the future, these energy developers feel such projects will continue to be essential. They would tend to agree with Exxon president Randall Meyers' statement to the 1980 American Mining Congress, as reported by the Associated Press (1980), that "... virtually all growth in domestic energy supply will have to come from conventional nuclear power and direct burning of fossil fuels." This means, he went on to say, major growth in synthetic fuels, especially processing coal and oil shale which would be concentrated in arid, sparsely populated parts of the west and would require the transport of water into the region in an amount estimated at two to four barrels for each barrel of oil produced from shale.

Those protesting such "hard path" energy facilities frequently display images of the smiling sun and whirring windmills to symbolize their preference for the small and the renewable -- the "soft path". They claim that only the soft, small, local and renewable will lead us away from environmental degradation and the loss of private land rights to those who use eminent domain to build the big systems. They warn that the big projects, especially nuclear energy facilities, will need to use police state tactics to build and maintain the big projects in the face of local resistance. Those protesting the big DC power line from North Dakota through west central Minnesota point to the way, for example, that first state police, then the Minnesota Bureau of Criminal Apprehension, and then the Federal Bureau of Investigation were brought in to control resistance to the line and eventually sabotage. These protesters pointed out that this DC power line should indeed be called an 800 kV DC system, emphasizing thereby their claim that one of the reasons it was a threat was that it was so large. They claimed that when the power cooperatives called it a ± 400 kV DC system, they were seeking to portray it as smaller than it really was. Antinuclear protesters who sometimes join in protesting such large power lines, or coal fired power plants, and are against all large scale energy development, quote German researcher Robert Jungck (1979) to show that the nuclear establishment across the world will build centralized totalitarian regimes or "the Atom Staat" as an inevitable part of their process of delivering energy from nuclear sources. They contrast this with the image of how self-reliant people working at the local level can design and develop energy to accord with the natural environment. Similarly, people, especially in rural areas, call for rapid development and marketing of alcohol fuels by small local cooperatives or just individual farmers to provide a reliable and self-reliant energy future, independent of big oil. They also criticize the efforts by large or specialized grain handling organizations to become the dominant producers of fuel alcohol, and argue that it is wrong that government gives these big operations financial support for such alcohol production instead of fostering the small and the local.

So it seems we have here a debate between two groups of people, each projecting a quite different, and indeed, rival design for the future, and the steps, or paths to take to get there. Indeed, the debate has become a kind of ideological and political war marked by the claim that only one side can or must win.

ANOTHER DUEL: SYSTEMIC INTERDEPENDENCE VERSUS LOCALIZED INDEPENDENCE

Now, if we think more carefully about this, especially if we turn back just a few years, we realize that people have also been debating the competing virtues and necessities of two other paths into the future. One is to find ways to manage the environment and the interaction of humans and environment as systems of tightly interdependent parts that, as John Muir put it, are all "hitched together" in a "holistic" way so that "you can't change just one thing," and thus that solutions cause problems. The other is to deal with problems one at a time, finding solutions one by one through specialist attack. This one problem, one solution approach, or what some have called the application of tunnel vision, has been the tried and true one in industrial society. Others have called it a kind of intellectual surgery, (De Jouvenel, 1970:105) cutting but one or two variables from a set of events and shunting aside the rest of the set as but externalities. I think that this approach retains its vitality, but has become much less fashionable to advocate. Indeed, there is a new way to attack it, as a newly established enemy which must be overcome. Attackers band systems thinkers as elitists who want to run everything from the top down. They call instead for a return to the traditional American values of preserving property rights, progress, local control and local independence. They say we must "get government off the backs of people" and get on with the business of developing resources to promote economic progress. This return to progress and local independence is then counter-attacked by both the systems thinkers or established environmentalists, and those who simply oppose specific development projects who either say this view reflects ignorance of the complex interdependence in natural systems or that it reflects the self-seeking, wheeling-dealing of developers conniving with the local power structure.

THE BATTLEFIELD

We see examples of these rival designs and debates in water and land cases, and in energy cases where people take opposing sides in struggles over development or redevelopment projects and management plans. In these, we see not only how the two sets of polar debates seem to contradict and cross cut each other, but we find that people use the seeming inconsistencies to achieve a multitude of purposes all along the range between the poles.

For example, people in a set of rural communities becoming new outliers of suburban development spreading out from the Twin Cities of Minneapolis and St. Paul opposed the construction of a central water system to supply the area's water and replace present dependence upon local wells. This project was planned in joint venture by four local governments and was endorsed by local business-commercial interests. The citizens complained on the one hand that this central water system would lay down the infrastructure which would promote more suburban growth in the area and, they claimed, thus endanger the quality of the semi-rural life they presently enjoyed. In connection with this, the protesters criticized the way local governments went to the federal government for financial aid to develop this central water project, and, indeed, argued that it was because a federal agency provided development funds in the first place that their government officials became interested in promoting the project. The plan was shaped in accordance with provisions of a federal agency grant program for emergency drought relief.

One of the protest strategies to stop the development of this central water system was to ask for intervention against it by the Metropolitan Council, a multi-county oversight organization whose purpose it is to help regulate and manage growth within the seven county metropolitan area, and treat it as an integrated system. The protesters complained that the project promoted urban sprawl in contravention of Metropolitan Council guidelines. The Council, for example, has sought to prevent extension of sewer systems into undeveloped areas to control growth and to concentrate it within sewer districts. Some people in the Council seemed interested in this central water system issue, and did seem to feel that it would be a key influence on growth. Legally, the Council could intervene since part of one of the communities in the project was in a county within its jurisdiction. Also, there had been talk of eventually extending this jurisdiction to adjacent counties as they grow and take on metropolitan characteristics. But as the Council was considering how it might intervene, the area within its jurisdiction was dropped from the water system project. The protesters felt that the promoters of the project decided to make the project smaller and to drop this particular area to avoid Council intervention. They continued to claim that the project should be examined and controlled because of its impact on the total metropolitan area as a system. One of their other arguments against the project was that their own individual wells were perfectly good and viable, and that they didn't need to be tied into a larger water system. As part of their legal battle against the project, they went to a district court to challenge the ways the local government committed their community to increased assessments to pay back some of the federal loan matching the federal development grant.

The promoters of the project were able to obtain federal funding because of the provisions of the Federal emergency drought relief program. They thus stressed the systemic nature of water flows within their area, the impact on this system of individual wells, and the unreliability of individual wells in the case of larger scale drought. They also argued that they had a duty to serve all the people, not just a few homeowners. The protesting homeowners argued that they weren't simply thinking of themselves, but about the impact on the whole area of the growth and development which would follow upon this large scale project. They claimed this project would primarily benefit local development and land interests. In this, they certainly did not share the sentiment voiced by proponents of decentralization and local control that local government is more trusted and trustworthy than "remote" regional or federal government. But they did find fault in the way a federal agency funded the project without examining its implications in this case, how project promoters and protesters both shifted their arguments concerning scale and level to suit practical purposes.

In many ways this case was similar to one on even a more local level, a case involving the repair of a drainage ditch in the northeast suburbs of the Twin Cities of Minneapolis and St. Paul, Minnesota. Local residents organized to oppose the ditch repair on the grounds that it would lower the level of the wildlife ponds in the area, impose assessments upon them, yet primarily benefit a land developer and some sod farmers. They said that the developers and the sod farmers control local government, and would use this and other projects to lower water tables so that more land could be developed for multiple housing. They opposed the approval of the ditch repair project by the local watershed board, again arguing that the members of the board were hand in glove with the developers. They have counter-attacked by bringing the case before state level agencies charged with controlling, regulating, and managing water and land resources, claiming that only at this level can decisions be made to protect the environment and also to bring objectivity and honesty to the decision process. Indeed, they have also sought to have legislation passed which essentially would make such ditch repair projects always require state level permits.

But the same kind of local people who, on the one hand, criticize local government as too easily manipulatable by local power elites, will on the other call for an end to the interference of Big Government. In the north-east area of the state, a broad range of citizens mobilized in what they called a "conservation alliance" to protest the ways the federal government expanded its rights and controls over local and adjacent waters in an area designated as the Boundary Waters Canoe Area (BWCA).

This case is one of many examples of large-small debates to be found in issues where some call for managing a body of water and adjoining land as a wilderness or a coastal zone in ways which greatly control or restrict individual or specific actions, emphasizing the complex and delicately balanced nature of the resource, while others resist this and emphasize the right of individuals to use the resource in many diverse ways according to local and individual custom instead of according to the dictates of external elites.

Perhaps the most well-known of such cases in the United States, the BWCA case, is similar to large energy cases in that managing this region of northeast Minnesota as a wilderness and canoe area also means that, like centralized energy projects, it is managed extensively, intensively, and with complex organization. These processes tend to fabricate or concentrate the resources of wilderness according to current human design and concept. Through involved federal legislation, it brings under the control of various federal bodies the regulation and management of an area which spreads across several counties and requires ongoing negotiated understandings with Canada, which borders the area and which governs use of a very similar or identical environment just across an imaginary border. Both countries must also deal with groups or tribes of American Indians living on both sides of the border who claim special considerations. This area is then to be managed carefully according to a defined formula to protect and enhance its wilderness aspects according to prevailing concepts about what constitutes wilderness -- human concepts, to be sure. For example, motors will be excluded from more, and eventually all, of it; areas of canoe use will be defined; the kinds of food which can be brought into it will be specified; also where and how people can camp in it, when and where they can use fire to cook food, where and when they can enter it, and in what numbers. A major purpose of this is to reduce over use and to allow those using it to feel that here is, indeed, an area untrammeled by the machines and domination of humankind, a type of "planned, spontaneous uniqueness."

This big project, extensive in its scope and proliferation of impacts, intensive in its requirements for planning and management, and complex in its provisions and organizational involvements, is not the work of big business putting profits over people and environment. Instead, it is in large part the work of the increasingly institutionalized environmental movement working through lawyers, lobbyists, and some party politicking to influence legislators. Such plans reflect an idea once all but limited to ecological or sociological specialists, or counter-cultural activists, that the environment is an ecological system whose complex interdependencies must be managed tightly and on large scale to protect it from the actions of individuals and local governments which are apparently perceived of as naturally unwise, unthinking, or selfish. A centralized, big project is called for to protect against the way scores, hundreds, or thousands of individual and local decisions and actions -- decentralized -- add up into a condition which is considered contrary to the public interest by other individuals who have clout because of the way they have mobilized in large scale interest groups and have influenced big centralized government.

This case throws more light on the large-small, centralized-decentralized, hard-soft debate, and helps show how complex it is. The environmentalists in this case call for the federal level, centralized control to protect a means of recreation and wilderness use which could well come under the category "soft". The users of this area temporarily seek to live close to nature, spending little at the moment, but bringing in foods elaborately made with space age technology. The canoes they use are increasingly improved, again using high technology, and people admire the technological advances found in the equipment used by each other. All of this is protested by people living nearby in the name of private ownership, local control, freedom of choice, and multiple use of public lands. Further, they warn that this legislative change will change the lifestyle of people living in the area's small towns, a lifestyle they have a right to enjoy, especially since they gave up the big jobs in the big cities to do it. They warn that this legislation will ruin the economy and hence the vitality of these small towns -- much the same argument made by the farmers and rural people fighting the DC power line or other groups fighting other large scale energy development.

We see similar kinds of at least seeming inconsistencies in ideology and action in a case which has come to be a kind of classic hard-soft, large-small energy war -- the protest against a large DC power line in Minnesota. In 1974, when the project was announced and the Rural Electric Cooperatives were working to negotiate with local landowners and governments to put the line through, protesting farmers demanded that it come under the new state siting act and thus be heard by a new state level board. The cooperatives argued that they were grandfathered out because the project had begun before the law took effect. But then when some local governments began siding with the protesters and threatened to try to "zone out" the line, the cooperatives agreed that it should come under the state process which seemed to promise a more timely granting of permits in one organized and centralized set of steps or process. The farmers initially welcomed this state intervention as it provided them a whole new forum to protest and it initially did delay construction. But when the state agencies, following some 18 months of deliberations, did determine the route and granted a construction permit, the farmers challenged this as more evidence of centralized decision making which erodes local rights even as it pushes through big energy projects. In the process, they began speaking and hearing about the concept that "small is beautiful" and that soft energy paths, decentralization and small scale solar development was a more appropriate approach than these big, hard, centralized efforts. In the process of fighting their case in the courts, one of their lawyers sought to bring it before federal courts and make of it a federal case, even as his clients were, in another context, calling for much more local control and were strongly objecting to the use of state police to prevent them from blocking construction. The line has been completed, but it has been plagued by sabotage, including actual felling of some of the pylons. This has led the cooperatives and the state to call for intervention by the Federal Bureau of Investigation to apprehend the saboteurs and protect the line. This intervention was accomplished through the legal step of turning ownership of the line over to the Federal Rural Electrification Administration. As could be expected, protesters feel this is an extreme case of moving energy development along the hard and centralized path, and some have increased their personal involvement in promotion of small scale solar development.

Clearly, the way citizens mobilize to block a project or plan, regardless of the resource focus, is by building a viable organization. Characteristically, they try to build a large organization which is as broadly based as they can make it, in order to challenge the project across as broad a front as possible. Even if they are calling for small, locally administered projects as an alternative to projects they oppose partly on the grounds that they are too large, they will want to build a big resistance effort. In the process of gaining legitimacy and bringing in allies, they will characteristically extend beyond the initial issue or focus of resistance to overlap in and join efforts with groups protesting other kinds of projects or promoting other causes.

Farmers blocking the ± 400 or 800 kV DC powerline built just this kind of organization. Groups sprang up in the communities across the nine Minnesota counties over which the line was to pass. Then, these resistance groups integrated in joint effort as, for example, they pooled their funds to obtain legal counsel, and to present their case against the project in public hearings and in the courts at district and state levels. Further, they allied, or tried to ally with groups fighting or questioning the same line in an adjoining state of North Dakota, and, indeed, tried to help promote groups to form opposition to the North Dakota portion of the line, and to join their alliance. Furthermore, they allied with groups fighting siting and construction of a 345 kV AC extension from this DC line into southern Minnesota, and they formed links with groups fighting other utilities building or planning to build other power lines in other counties or in other states. Then they began to forge links with groups opposing large scale energy projects generally, across the country. For example, they have tied into networks of anti-nuclear groups, especially one in Minnesota, and anti-surface mining groups, especially one based in Montana. Finally, they have also formed links with groups, organizations, or individuals calling for the development of small scale and locally controlled solar energy projects. The more widespread and diffuse their alliances, the more they stress the ideology that they are working for a soft path, the small, the renewable, and the decentralized or local, and that they are working against the hard path, the large, and centralized. The more that they stress these polar extremes, the more they argue in terms of the need for fundamental change in our lifestyle as we make a jump to a new energy future.

Alliance building also occurs across issues. For example, the Conservation Alliance protesting the new BWCA legislation searched for allies first among groups concerned about other water or land control plans, such as conversion by the state of abandoned railway right of ways to public trails, or designation of rivers or streams as wild and scenic, or new wilderness designations in Alaska, but then also found common cause with those protesting the large DC powerline in Minnesota. The issue of eminent domain was one concern they had in common, but they also came to understand that they were all little people, just plain home folks, standing against injustice. They called their new coalition "Minnesotans for Equitable Government" and, by government, they implied powerful authorities of all types.

In the process of these efforts at alliance building and extension of ideology, some of the local protest groups diminished in size, but generally it can be said that they grew in ideological concern, in the scope of protest, and in the range of interests. They did so by building social networks rather than by widening the base of a top-down, pyramidal organization. I have elsewhere described in great detail that in their growth, protest organizations tend to be segmentary, or composed of many groups, polycentric, or having many leaders, but are integrated in a network composed of interweaving and overlapping groups and often crisscrossing of leaders who move about somewhat like circuit riding evangelists (Gerlach, 1971; Gerlach and Palmer, 1980; Gerlach and Radcliffe, 1979). This type of organization mobilizes enough large-scale power to challenge established orders, but still provides necessary flexibility for the tactical maneuvering which is so adaptive in resource disputes with big industry or big government.

Industry also knows how to use size, scale, and organization in flexible ways to adapt to different situations both in its conflict with protest groups, its negotiations with government, and its response to government regulations. On the one hand, it now must be painfully aware that the larger scale of the project, the more likely it is to meet with effective resistance by grassroots groups which come together in the large scale networks described above. Perhaps the major weakness of the ± 400 kV DC powerline with its 345 kV AC extension was that because of its length, it could stimulate resistance by different groups over so large an area. Further, the larger the project is, the easier it is for groups to find common ideological cause to come together against it. If nothing else, the large-small debate has put large on the defensive. But on the other hand, large size carries with it some advantages. Even though ideological support for large may somewhat be muted or on the defensive, there probably still is a general view that the only way we are going to solve our energy problems is by doing things on a big enough scale, using state-of-the-art technology. It may not be fashionable to pronounce this in hearings involving people resisting the big projects around the banner of "small is more beautiful," but the concept probably remains part of dominant American culture.

More obviously, large and complex projects involving many interests with many beneficiaries -- for example, a multi-county powerline project linked to a large power plant serving various states, feeding into regional and national grids, and involving the joint ventures of large energy, financial, and industrial organizations -- can have an advantage by seeming so big that potential protesters will feel that it simply is unrealistic to try to stop it. Often in our research we have heard people say "if they want to build this thing, they will do it." Further, once such a large project starts mobilizing capital, spending funds, hiring people, and building things, it gives so many areas, peoples, and interest groups an economic or political stake in the project that they will worry about their own futures if it is stopped. This was one of the arguments presented by the builders of the contested ± 400 kV DC line against a proposed moratorium on the project to reconsider health and safety impacts in the face of growing militant farmer resistance. Similar arguments have been used in West Germany by builders of a contested nuclear power plant at Grohnde near Hameln in Lower Saxony, again against a suit that progress on construction on the plant be halted while more impact studies on the project were conducted.

But the same large size can become a liability if the project is, in fact, stymied during development, since any delay can tie up so much capital so often borrowed at high interest and since it can affect so many. One of the reasons a large project can be stymied is, indeed, because somewhere over the broad scope of its operations, it is likely to be vulnerable to some type of protest by one of many different groups which have a stake in resisting it. Somewhere in so large a project, there can be found some legal reason to question it in the courts or in hearings, for example, on the grounds that it has contravened some environmental or procedural regulation. For example, even though the ± 400 kV DC portion of the above mentioned power line has been completed, the 345 kV AC segment is tied up because the state supreme court found that affected farmers along the 345 kV AC corridor were not given notice of hearings concerning need for the project. The protesters across the length of the whole system are emboldened by this recent ruling to consider resurrecting their legal attack on the rest of the system. This ruling gives them a reason to again challenge the entire project since the builders originally claimed that need for 1000 megawatts was predicated on the assumption that the 345 kV AC and the ± 400 kV DC power lines were all part of the same system. Further, this ruling probably gives more legitimacy to those who feel that they must continue their fight against the line even if it means resorting to protest in the fields.

Another reason large size can become a liability is that government characteristically tightens control and regulations and brings projects which exceed a certain size under the scrutiny of public hearings, a costly and time-consuming process.

One way of escaping this liability is to build facilities small enough so that they are below the threshold at which they must be subject to certain critical evaluations in hearings. In Minnesota, for example, it is not necessary to obtain a certificate of need through the Minnesota Energy Agency need hearings in order to seek permission to build power plants under 50 megawatts, power lines under 200 kV or shorter than 100 miles within the state. Nor is it necessary to go through state siting hearings through the Environmental Quality Board for power plants under 50 megawatts, or power lines under 200 kV.

But the public has now become sufficiently sensitized to the problems of the big and the virtues of the small and local that the former are far more likely to have to be on the defensive while the latter are more likely to be accepted without much argument. For at least these reasons, industry will emphasize that projects are large for some purposes, but small for others, or will put forward projects of integrated wholes for some purposes while dividing them into components for other purposes -- that is, as tactical advantage indicates. For example, a rural electric cooperative association might emphasize for some purposes that it is now large, modern, staffed by trained professional experts, and able to compete with the biggest firms in the country for finances or credit. But for other purposes, it will emphasize that it is no more than a loose collection of really quite independent, locally managed cooperatives, run by boards of ordinary people so that it reflects the concerns and the votes of plain home folks. The local member cooperatives stress their independence as locally owned, citizen-based cooperatives when they ask why people would want to protest a facility built to serve them. But they also will often say that local costs of electric power are primarily a function of wholesale prices caused by the need of the wholesale supplier to pay for the big new facility which has been built based upon decisions and problems perceived years ago. They say they really have no control over these wholesale prices, and are simply small elements in the big systems of decisions made in the past, or, perhaps made at the federal or the international level.

In short, protesters, developers, citizens and officials move back and forth from pole to pole in ways which certainly make sense from a standpoint of practical adaptation and pragmatic political action, even though they don't fit the idealogical model that it is either hard or soft, large or small, local or central. What is is what works. Examples of this strategy are also found on the level of the individual. People who call for mass transit systems to replace the private automobile and thereby fight smog and save gas may well, on the other hand, call for small household level solar water heating systems to replace reliance on electricity or gas from large-scale, centralized production and distribution systems. Some will not take kindly to the proposition that use of the automobile also represents a small scale individualized technology which can be used decentrally. The problem lies not simply in the size of the technology, but in the ways many individual decisions to use it can add up to create a large scale problem for the total system. Solutions to such macro problems are likely to be sought in some type of large scale and coordinated control mechanisms. For example, we see this in the way people, who praise the virtues of wood as a fuel which gives them individual energy independence, join in calling for county or state government to regulate the way firewood wholesalers or lumber companies cut wood, and to control the type of wood cut or the type of combustion systems used by people so that they are both efficient and nonpolluting.

Some observers might find these shifts and flexes inconsistent enough to spin the head. Others will realize that such involvement in activities which seem mutually incompatible and ideologically inconsistent are understandable as the maneuverings of practical politics. Certainly, those involved in the events, sharing and shifting in ideology, seem to know their way through the maze. It makes sense to them. It just does not accord with the polarity principles pronounced by those who feel that we are at some kind of fundamental fork in the cultural and ecological road, and that it is either one way or another for people or for society as a whole. And it does not accord with the idea that people can´t cope with inconsistency and change.

BEYOND THE WARS: LEAP TO A WHOLE NEW ERA?

Now, it is the stock in trade of those called "futurists" to proclaim that this or that society is changing so radically that even its near term future will be fundamentally different from its present, and it seems that there is a ready audience for this message. An aide to a senator from Minnesota is so concerned that the large-small hard-soft debate represents a watershed in American life that he seems anxious to assure that his senator is on the cresting wave. A major investor-owned electric utility in the upper Northwest became noted through the industry and around the communities it serves for the way it used audio-visual materials to demonstrate that the United States was indeed at a point of transformation so that the old rules and concepts guiding the energy industry and, indeed, other industries, were suddenly being challenged and rejected, seemingly in favor of concepts favoring controlled growth. This view saw big energy industry as a threat and challenged the ethic of profit maximization while calling for broader corporate attention to social concerns and social responsibility.

Certainly futurists quote each other on this subject of transformation, as graphically illustrated in the papers presented at the "First Global Conference on the Future" held in Toronto, Canada in July, 1980, sponsored by the World Future Society and the Canadian Futures Society (Feather, 1980). It is also fashionable to describe the transformation as a process of paradigm transformation, following the stimulus of philosopher Thomas Kuhn (1962) who used paradigm to refer to the complete system of thought, rules of evidence, and means and criteria for criticism and measurement which characterized scientific theory. Kuhn tells us how one scientific theory occasionally pushes aside and succeeds another in the process of scientific advance. This concept of paradigm shift and revolution in scientific thought seems to approximate nicely the concept that there can be fundamental revolution in the way social cultural systems work; that is, a shift from one way of cultural thinking and social action to another. Thus, just as Amory Lovin's (1977) "soft energy path" is the flag to follow in arguing the need for a certain kind of shift in how we get and use energy, so is Kuhn's work the banner behind which a wave of futurists speak of cultural transformation, or rather, cultural paradigm shift. It probably should be added that while Lovins is an evangelist-advocate, Kuhn is much more just a scholar whose seminal ideas are used in successive reinterpretations, even though he himself questions these ideas in later publications, as scientists are wont to do. Minimally, Kuhn gave us some new tools to think about what sociologists or anthropologists might treat as problems in the maintenance or change of a socio-cultural system and, minimally, Lovins gave us some tools to think about and legitimate alternatives to a presently conventional and dominant sub-system of energy production and use. But what about the way people have bandwagoned on these themes? Experience tells us to be skeptical. Certainly, it is useful to distinguish between a system which is more or less stable, and unchanging, and a system which is changing in major, or should we say, revolutionary, ways. Probably it is useful to consider that these represent opposing poles on a continuum of change. In a previous work, I and Virginia Hine (1973) focused on distinguishing between what we called developmental change and revolutionary change. By developmental change we meant something more than simply maintaining the status quo, but much less than fundamental or revolutionary change. This has been called system change by some and is what Boulding calls a "system-break." We used the term developmental change to refer to change which keeps the established system alive by patching and repairing it, and by fine-tuning it. For example, we felt that within the total American socio-cultural system, getting rid of the private automobile, related sprawling residence patterns, polycentric shopping centers and long distance commuting would be revolutionary. In contrast, keeping the automobile alive through technological change such as improving the car's pollution control systems and significantly improving gas mileage would be developmental change. Similarly, a change for the Digo people of Kenya whom I studied from 1958 to 1960, replacing beliefs and spirits as causal agents of illness with belief in the germ theory and the power of Western medicine would be revolutionary. Related to this, adding Islamic ideas about spirit forces or jini to the complex of traditional spirits to improve ability to combat spirit-caused illness would be developmental change, while pushing aside the spirit complex and its practitioners called aganga with western medicine and its doctors would be revolutionary.

In our 1973 book, we saw modernization or westernization as a process which often brought fundamental change by bringing in new concepts about life and behavior, new rules of evidence to test and prove these concepts, and new systems of action. With this in mind, one of the questions we then asked was whether the ecology movement along with its concepts about systems and ideas about "you can't change just one thing" and also the no-growth movement with ideas that resources are limited and humans should live within, rather than over, the environment, were not best looked at as revolutionary cultural concepts which in turn act as kinds of guides or blueprints to social action challenging economic development projects.

But even as we were positing these essentially either-or propositions, I had my doubts. For example, I found it useful to discuss the 16th century and the period when the Protestant movement was on the rise as a time of fundamental change, which brought forth, as one analyst said, "a new heaven and a new earth" (Smith, 1966). But the more I thought about it, the more I discussed it with students and colleagues, the more I wondered whether the Protestant movement was not simply part of a longer wave of change which really made its big leap when technologies of the industrial age were produced. Recently, chemist-systems thinker Cesare Marchetti (1977) has argued that the great transformation we know as the rise of the industrial era began with the revolution in ideas brought into being with the rise and spread of Christianity which in turn has its roots in Judaism. These revolutionary ideas included that God created the world for man to use and dominate, the perception of time as open-ended which undergirds a concept of purposefulness and inevitable progress, and the notion that manual labor is good and wholesome. Right or wrong, his argument demonstrates or helps demonstrate that while many people believe that there are times when leaps are made from one era to another, they differ greatly on the time table. Further, just as some authors push back the time at which they think the great leap forward was made, others keep reminding us how the old lives on in the new (Kroeber, 1963). If we look, we certainly can see the pre-protestant elements in post-Reformation Europe, and elements of Ancient China, for example its authoritarian bureaucracy, in Communist China. And now, will current happenings in China and in Iran be interpreted as new revolutions or transformations which launched people from paths considered revolutionary when they were taken in the 1940s and 50s?

There are circumstances when it does seem quite useful to speak about the great change from hunting-gathering to agricultural ways of life, and then from agriculture to industry as times of great transformation. Nowadays, futurists like to do this as they urge us to be ready for a next great leap, or "wave" as Toffler (1980) calls it, which will carry us into yet another way of life. But again, it is not so easy to be sure where the great breaking points were or are. For example, the case study approach of modern empirical anthropology shows us how some people have transformed from being sedentary farmers to being hunters and gatherers. For example, Hoebel (1960) explains why the Cheyenne did this as, on the one hand, their sedentary, horticultural lifestyle was threatened by intertribal warfare and resource disputes, and on the other hand as the horse was introduced and the new resource of buffalo was made available to them. Incidentally, in his analysis, Hoebel gives us evidence to consider that this shift to hunting and gathering led the Cheyenne to fundamental change, but he also shows how much of the old Cheyenne way carried on into the new. In short, data and theory now lead me to be very skeptical about pronouncing this or that event, or this or that era to be one of great transformation, and therefore I feel we must treat with great skepticism the premise that the hard-soft debate does bring us to a point at which we must and will choose between two quite different ways of life.

Another premise could be that all of the apparent manipulation of the hard-soft debate, as we have described it in the cases summarized above, simply represent attempts by people to hide the fact that we are at a watershed since they don't want to take the ultimate but necessary plunge. It looks as if we are able to swing back and forth between hard and soft, because we are trying to perform the impossible of having our cake and eating it too. Lovins (1977) seems to reflect this view when he says that we simply don't have the resources to pursue both paths at the same time. I can't comment on the economic and technological feasibility of going two or more ways at once, although I suspect that selection and interpretation of these "hard" facts represents adherence to or rejection of the social cultural argument that there are limits to growth and we are now reaching them. But, is it socially, culturally and psychologically possible that people can simultaneously pursue so many paths into so many different possible futures? Will this manipulation of multiple options confuse and disorient people and lead many or most to what anthropologists and psychologists call anomie, or normlessness (Chinoy, 1961:362) because they in fact have too many contradictory norms?

Consistency or Diversity?

Just as the scholarly and popular literature is filled with propositions about times of great transformation, so is it filled with propositions that people do have trouble living with the contradictions brought into their lives by waves of radical change. Alvin Toffler (1971) grabbed public attention by arguing that as we move into a future so fundamentally different from our present or past, we will experience future shock. Zbigniew Brezezinski (1970), for example, argues that our social, political, and economic troubles have come about primarily because we are caught between two different ages: an old established industrial one dominated and run by a few great powers, and a new technetronic one in which new social political forces are in contest. Brezezinski quotes the novelist Hermann Hesse to express vividly the pathologies of living in such a state of confusion: "Human life is reduced to real suffering, to hell, only when two ages, two cultures and religions overlap... There are times when a whole generation is caught in this way between two ages, two modes of life, with the consequences that it loses all power to understand itself and has no standard, no security, no simple acquiescence." (from Steppenwolf). Another novelist, Robert Ruark (1976), portrays the Kikuyu people in the 1950s as suffering so badly from being caught between their old ways and values, and the new ways and values brought by the West which dominated them, that they launched the Mau Mau movement to destroy the contradictions and reestablish a less confusing and more integrated world based on old values. Eric Hoffer (1951, 1963) feels that people become so confused by being exposed to contradictory ideas caused by the ordeal of rapid change that they turn to charismatic leaders to give them a single new "true belief." This is not unlike the work of anthropologists Ralph Linton

(1943) and Anthony F. C. Wallace (1966) who explain in detail, enriched by case studies, how people impacted by forces of change experience such a disorientation and anomie or confusion of norms that they turn to movements they identify as revivalistic or nativistic to return them to a golden age or carry them towards a new vision.

Other scholars, especially anthropologists, have told us much about how societies tend towards establishing and maintaining social order and cultural consistency so that various beliefs and actions reinforce and support each other rather than conflict with each other (Hoebel, 1976; Fallers, 1960). In selecting new elements brought to them by contact with other people, developed within their own culture through social movements or other innovative mechanisms, people normally pick those which tend to fit the old ways, or they reinterpret both old and new so that they do tend to fit together in various new syntheses (Herskovits, 1947). This process of reworking and blending has been likened to a chemical fusion more than simply mechanical adding (Malinowski, 1938; Greenberg, 1946). It is in these terms, for example, that Greenberg explains how the Hausa people of northern Nigeria work Islam into their lives.

To be sure, these anthropologists are talking chiefly about change coming through contact among cultures, but the same models can be applied to change brought about from within the culture such as by a social movement like the environmental movement or its no-growth or pro-soft aspects, as we have demonstrated elsewhere (Gerlach and Hine, 1973). But how can soft blend with large? How can no-growth blend with growth? How can centralized blend with decentralized? Perhaps what we now see is simply some period of transition in which the reinterpreting and reworking is going on so that in time we will see some new kind of synthesis relatively free of contradiction and controversy. Perhaps this is what people in the conventional energy industry have in mind when they call for a mix of energy technologies. They are always careful to say that surely small scale solar will have its place in this mix, which, however, they feel will long be dominated by the larger and more conventional fossil and nuclear systems.

However, if we explore the anthropological literature further, we see that there is some significant criticism of the consistency model. There is enough theory and enough case study evidence to indicate that a people can live with many quite contradictory patterns of cultural concept and social action, and that indeed, there are times when they reach out to bring in contradiction to expand the range of choice making and manipulation open to them. Robert Murphy (1971), for example, says that there is considerable variation and conflict among cultural parts, between norms and actions, because society and individuals have contradictory requirements. People with this viewpoint don't agree that this confusion or contradiction is simply a temporary state between normal periods of tight integration, but they see it as the normal way society works, and, indeed, the way it makes change. In presenting this view, E. R. Leach (1970) draws his immediate evidence from the way some peoples in the hill country of northeast Burma lived simultaneously as members of two supposedly quite different and distinct cultural systems: the Kachin and the Shan. Officially, according to the Burmese government and the conventional scholarly assessment of geographers, the Shans occupy the river valleys, cultivate rice on a large scale on irrigated fields under relatively centralized economic and political direction, and have a culture much like the ruling Burmese with a feudal hierarchy. In contrast, the Kachins live in the hills where they use slash and burn technology and shifting cultivation to grow dry rice on what can be called small scale. Their communities are essentially democratic and egalitarian. What Leach shows us is that in fact many people in the Burmese hills can be said to be simultaneously Kachin and Shan, shifting frequently and easily, back and forth, between these contradictory worlds to achieve political, economic and social objectives in each. Further, by moving between these polar opposites, they may achieve a variety of cultural blendings and combine patterns from each. For the sake of analysis, Leach identified the most common cluster of compromise patterns as the Gumsa system. But he emphasizes that Gumsa does not represent the single new system which is emerging from the syntheses of these contradictory possibilities. If anything, this seems to mean that these people have three rather clear paradigms, and also everything in between. These people signal which cultural world or mix of worlds they are occupying at any one time by the language they use, the dress they wear, or the religion they practice. But they can easily display all of these patterns or varying syntheses of them. In this they certainly seem similar to North Americans who move freely between arguments for the hard or the soft, the systemic or the lineal paradigms.

Similar flexibility is displayed by the Digo people of the Kenya coast. The Digo also moved easily among a number of worlds. In their traditional social structure, the right to manage key property such as valuable coconut plantations, and the duty to care for kin descends matrilineally, that is from mother to daughter or especially from mother's brother to sister's son. Traditional Digo religion centered around belief in a multitude of spirit forces which they sought to control through traditional ritual. The Digo were essentially egalitarian and democratic with local communities existing quite independently one of another, each governed by councils of relatively equal elders. They grow corn, casava, and some dry rice by slash and burn techniques and shifting cultivation. Officially, the Digo converted to Islam, and accepted much Arab-Islamic culture. With this came patrilineal inheritance, and emphasis on participating in trading systems in which the main aim is to maximize profit instead of sharing production or profits with kin folk, their traditional way of redistributing wealth and leveling entrepreneurship. In the late 1950s and early 60s when I studied their way of life, Digo did live simultaneously in these various worlds, using these competing paradigms. That is, they moved freely back and forth between being very traditional Digo and highly Islamicized Digo, or various forms in between. This meant, for example, that when a man died, both his sons (including his brother's sons) and his sister's sons had equal but contradictory rights to his property according to competing principles, one patrilineal and Islamic, and one matrilineal and traditional. The British colonial government felt that this led to confusion, as demonstrated by the many conflict cases over inheritance in the local, and, indeed, often higher level courts. To help the Digo "make up their mind" and get regularity in the law, the British wanted the Digo to determine which was the one proper way and stick to it. But the Digo wanted the contradictions. With them they could arrive at the best combination for any given situation. And, indeed, if that combination later did not work, they could reconsider it using a competing rule. Characteristically they would select the person or persons best able to manage property on very pragmatic grounds of demonstrated ability. Sometimes they established a new system where many different, but competing heirs shared equally, and then in respect to this cooperated in other ways. The components of such compromise groups varied considerably from case to case and did not represent an emergent social structure, but simply another set of alternatives. As in the Kachin-Shan case, the Digo and their interacting neighbors used language and religious expression to symbolize the system or option they were using at any one time. They used the traditional Digo language to indicate old ways of redistributing property matrilineally, or of sharing gains among kin. They used Swahili to defend patrilineal inheritance or to conduct trade or commerce. Thus, a Digo merchant might say in Swahili that in business, there is no mother's brother, but use the Digo language when participating in traditional spirit-centered ceremonials in which successful Digo shared with their less successful matrilineal kin.

MANY CRISSCROSSING PATHS

All the evidence is that people can live in many cultural worlds, or paradigms; that they are not confused by the inconsistencies among these opposing ways, but, indeed, gain the flexibility they want by keeping both polar ends available as well as many options in between. Now, it might well be asked, why don't people simply drop the labels like Kachin and Shan; Digo and Arab; or hard or soft paths. Why don't they simply say: "Take that which is best and most pragmatic at a given moment." Labeling both established and alternative patterns and supporting these labels with symbols gives people a chance to conceptualize and then manipulate them more effectively, to play them off against each other, to achieve a broader range of options. Thus, the labeling continues even when the new alternative becomes well-entrenched.

Some scholars, notably Claude Levi-Strauss (1936:86-7 & 132-163) feel that it is inherent in the nature of the human mind that humans speak in terms of binary opposition, and that in time this is reflected in the characteristic way duality and structural opposition is built into most social systems. Perhaps, but we need not turn to this search for root causes to explain what happens in the cases we have been discussing. We have seen that the reasons are more overt: people simply find it convenient to manipulate extremes to achieve a broader field for more flexible maneuver.

Some philosophers, notably William Irwin Thompson (1978), use Eastern philosophy to argue that life is characterized by a constant movement of opposites in which Yin and Yang oppose, but complement each other to achieve a middle harmony, but in the cases we have been examining, there seems to be less an interest in achieving a middle path than in widening the distance between the poles and opposition.

The Peltos (1976) give us a useful tool for understanding the function of widening the poles. Using ideas from John Roberts and Ward Goodenough (1971), they speak of three levels of culture. One is the culture carried and used by individuals. Another is the public culture which comes about in daily life as individuals interact, work out the most adaptive and mutually acceptable patterns, and assure that most people adhere to the prevailing public culture so that each can predict what the other will do. The third level of culture is what they call the culture pool which, following the analogy of the gene pool, consists of all the cultural possibilities -- that is the full inventory of possibilities known to a people at any time. Culture serves as a non-genetic, adaptive system because it guides and gives predictability to individuals so that they can work together to solve problems and pass on these solutions to new generations. It provides enough variation and diversity from which to select new generations, new possibilities, meet new problems, or extend adaptive strategies. Cultural invention, including such new cultural ideas as shifting to a soft path, can be compared to new genetic possibilities emerging through mutation or cross fertilization.

In our own system, which has developed powerful and, indeed, dominant patterns around large-scale technology, centrally coordinated decision making, emphasis on economic growth, and increasing reliance on ever more extensive, but also more complex interdependence, it seems adaptive to add, in a growingly powerful and legitimate way, the alternatives now called soft. That is, it seems useful to invent and apply new small technologies, redirect more decision making at the local level, seek areas where greater local self-sufficiency can be achieved, and experiment with ways to control growth and cope with the results of control. If these alternatives were simply proposed as possible by a few members of a society, they wouldn't have the power or legitimacy to extend the cultural range in a viable way any more than if some Digo would simply say let's consider letting sons inherit property. Such ideas would not likely be conceptualized, talked about, or even identified as important possibilities by established decision-makers, or by ordinary people, by teachers or by students, nor would they be communicated by the mass media. Instead, they would be ignored or ridiculed. To be considered eventually as major legitimate alternatives, it seems they must be presented as <u>the</u> major new path, the only right path to move into a new age.

The ideology of right versus wrong then, is used to legitimate consideration of pathways otherwise ignored or rejected. But once these are legitimated as alternatives, few want to close out the other routes. It does not matter that specialists will argue that in this world of limits it is necessary to close some routes to open others. Ordinary people will do to the idea of limits what they do to the idea that there is a best type of technology or level of decision-making. They will want it all. They will call for no-growth for some purposes and growth for others, soft for some, hard for others, local decision making for some, and higher levels for others. What is logically inconsistent or impure to the specialist makes sense to people working their way through the multichannel maze of life. We see this not only in our culture and our era, but across cultures and history. In the world of Islam, for example, prophets and lawyers were the specialists who proclaimed that people must leave old ways and get on the true path, the <u>Sharia</u> (Gibb, 1962; Levy, 1957; Fyzee, 1949; Schacht, 1950). But closer examination shows that such prophets and lawyers each defined different paths as the only right one and in the process helped legitimate many different ones. Ordinary people, in turn, did their own picking, choosing, and blending of old ways and new options to create their own syntheses. What has emerged are broad avenues and winding paths as Islam has grown, and in turn influenced other peoples. Also, consider Martin Luther's attempt to reform the church, to set it back on the true path. It led not simply to two possible routes, the Catholic or the Protestant, but to many different paths, crisscrossing, shifting, dividing again and again, and converging. It made things very untidy for some of the social map makers, but it gave people many options. This increase in flexibility may have been as important in promoting the rise of industrial culture as anything else -- no single jump to a new path, no riding a single new wave, but many different waves. The convergences and divergences continue, confusing those who keep looking for simple bifurcation.

Now, if we look again at the propositions made by Thomas Kuhn (1962), we note that while he discusses how in the physical sciences one paradigm can emerge to contest and then displace another, he also explains that in the social sciences a number of opposing paradigms can co-exist at any time, in part because none clearly disproves any other. Interestingly, those futurists who refer to Kuhn's idea of scientific revolution to support their premise that we are experiencing a revolution in social-cultural paradigms seem to ignore his description of how social science paradigms co-exist. In explaining to students why there are so many competing theories to explain and analyze behavior in social events, and, indeed, so many contradictory uses of the same terms or why so often many different terms are used to label the same event, we frequently say that situations and objectives can dictate the theory or the terminology one uses. It seems logical to extend this argument to explain why and how people use so many competing and contradictory cultural premises or social forms.

We see an interesting example of this in the way the auto industry straddles the large-small debate and communicates its composite answer to the public. Cadillac offers a car which ranges easily with the press of an accelerator from four to six to eight cylinders. The driver can adapt to any traffic condition effortlessly, calling on just the right amount of power for the situation, and is aided in this by the operation of an on-board computer. The driver can be soft and gas-saving or hard and commanding according to the situation. All the options are there, instead of a single possibility. It seems symbolic of the approach Americans, and, indeed, many people, like best.

While futurists speak of a paradigm shift, people are shifting among paradigms. While purists condemn such shifting as a kind of backsliding or wheeling-dealing, and while some psychologists and some social and behavioral scientists worry about the way people can cope with the shock of rapid change and the confusion of norms, people use polar debates as they are now using the hard-soft, large-small debate to achieve the flexibility through diversity necessary to cope with change and uncertainty in the availability and use of key resources.

REFERENCES

Associated Press. 1980. Report on 1980 American Mining Congress. Minneapolis Tribune, May 6, 1980.

Brezezinski, Zbigniew. 1970. Between Two Ages: America's Role in the Technetronic Era. New York: The Viking Press.

Chinoy, Ely. 1961. Society. New York: Random House, Inc.

De Jouvenel, Bertrand. 1970. "The Stewardship of the Earth." In Smithsonian Annual Symposium, 1967 Proceedings, The Fitness of Man's Environment. New York: Harper Colophon Books, Harper and Row.

Fallers, Lloyd. 1960. "Predicament of the Modern African Chief: An Instance From Uganda." In Simon and Phoebe Ottenberg (eds), Cultures and Societies of Africa: 504-521. New York: Random House.

Feather, Frank (ed). 1980. Through the 80's: Thinking Globally, Acting Locally. Washington, D.C.: World Future Society.

Fyzee, A.A.A. 1949. Outlines of Muhammadan Law. London: Oxford University Press.

Goodenough, Ward. 1971. Culture, Language and Society. Module 7. Reading, Pennsylvania: Addison-Wesley.

Gerlach, Luther P. 1971. "Movements of Revolutionary Change: Some Structural Characteristics." American Behavioral Scientist, 14(6):812-836.

Gerlach, Luther P. and Virginia H. Hine. 1973. Lifeway Leap: The Dynamics of Change in America. Minneapolis: University of Minnesota Press.

Gerlach, Luther P. and Gary B. Palmer. 1980. "Global Adaptation Through Evolving Interdependence." In William Starbuck and Paul C. Nystrom (eds.), Handbook of Organizational Design. New York: Oxford Press.

Gerlach, Luther P. and Betty Radcliffe. 1979. "Can Independence Survive Interdependence?" Futurics, 3(3):181-206.

Gibb, H.A.R. 1962. Mohammedanism. New York: Oxford University Press.

Greenberg, Joseph. 1946. The Influence of Islam on a Sudanese Religion. Seattle: University of Washington Press.

Herskovits, Melville. 1947. Man and His Works. New York: Alfred H. Knopf.

Hoebel, E. Adamson, and Everett L. Frost. 1976. Cultural and Social Anthropology. New York: McGraw-Hill Book Company.

Hoebel, E. Adamson. 1960. The Cheyenne: Indians of the Great Plains. New York: Holt, Rinehart and Winston.

Hoffer, Eric. 1957. The True Believer. New York: Harper and Row.

Hoffer, Eric. 1963. The Ordeal of Change. New York: Harper and Row.

Jungck, Robert. 1979. The New Tyranny: How Nuclear Power Enslaves Us. New York: Fred Jordan Books/Grosset and Dunlap.

Kroeber, A.J. 1963. Anthropology: Culture Patterns and Processes. New York: Harcourt Brace Jovanovich.

Kuhn, Thomas. 1962. The Structure of Scientific Revolutions. Chicago: University of Chicago Press.

Leach, E.R. 1970. Political Systems of Highland Burma: A Study of Kachin Social Structure. London, England: University of London, The Athlone Press. (Reprinted first edition - G. Bell and Son, Ltd., 1954).

Levi-Strauss, Claude. (Translated by Claire Jacobsen and Brooke Grundfest Schoepf) 1963. Strucutural Anthropology. New York: Basic Books, Inc.

Levy, Reuben. 1957. The Social Structure of Islam. Cambridge, England: University Press.

Linton, Ralph. 1943. "Nativistic Movements." American Anthropologist, 45:230-240.

Lovins, Amory B. 1977. Soft Energy Paths: Towards a Durable Peace. Harmondsorth, England: Penguin Books.

Malinowski, B. 1938. "Introductory Essay on the Anthropology of Changing African Cultures." In International Institute of African Language and Cultures, Methods of Study of Culture Contact in Africa. Oxford University Press, Memorandum XV, pp vii-xxxviii.

Marchetti, Cesare. 1977. "On Progress and Providence" In House Professional Paper. Laxenburg, Austria: Institute for Applied Systems Analysis.

Murphy, Robert F. 1971. The Dialectics of Social Life. New York: Basic Books.

Pelto, Gretel H. and Pertti J. 1976. The Human Adventure: An Introduction to Anthropology. New York: Macmillan, Inc.

Ruark, Robert J. 1976. Something of Value. Englewood Cliffs, New Jersey: Prentice Hall.

Schacht, J. 1950. The Origins of Muhammadan Jurisprudence. London: Oxford University Press.

Smith, Preserved. 1966 Reformation in Europe. New York: Colier Books. (First printing 1922 by Henry Holt & Co.)

Thompson, William Irwin. 1978. Darkness and Scattered Light: Four Talks on the Future. Garden City, New York: Anchor Books.

Toffler, Alvin. 1980. The Third Wave. New York: William Morrow & Co.

Toffler, Alvin. 1971. Future Shock. New York: Bantam.

Wallace, A.F.C. 1966. Religion: An Anthropological View. New York: Random House.

Part 3

Action Programs

Steven Ferrey

5. Building an Equitable Solar Future: A Primer on How Not to Bungle the Energy Transition

SOLAR THROUGH A NEW LENS

We need a new vision of solar energy. When we think of renewable energy and its impacts, we conceptualize solar technologies in terms of components and hardware, and we see their impacts on a very grand and global scale. Of course solar energy is delivered to consumers through hardware and technology. Moreover, its potential and impacts truly are sweeping -- conserving vast quantities of energy, reducing environmental degradation and leading to softer energy paths. While these conceptualizations are indeed a valid means to understand the importance of renewable energy systems, they do not provide a sharp insight as to the making of the solar transition, nor of the potential impacts of these technologies on individuals, institutions, and particularly, urban regions.

What I submit is necessary, is to view solar through a different lens. If we focus on how we make the solar transition -- who benefits, who pays, the interface with existing energy systems -- we will perceive a much different view of the role of renewable energy systems and the role of government in determining the fabric of our society. In one sense, we must focus on more discreet and disaggregated facets of the use of solar technologies. In these discreet examinations will be found, I believe, many of the answers which are required if we are to plan and shape the transition to renewables in a manner which best exploits both the technological potential of design and hardware and equitably serves the needs of all citizens. There are four axes along which I will grind this new lens.

1. <u>Solar Must Be Conceptualized Not As Merely A Technological Entity, But As A Marketing Phenomenon</u>

We have become most comfortable with the scientific aspects of renewable technologies. We have studied media of heat transfer, the absorptive and reflective qualities of a multitude of materials, the crystalline structure of photovoltaics. These aspects are hard and precise. We have not paid as much attention to the means by which solar will be promoted, subsidized and marketed. What are the developmental implications of certain renewable technologies maturing more quickly than others? Which individuals, institutions and regions will have access to renewables? How will decentralized sources interface with existing utility services? What is the appropriate scale on which to develop renewables? We do not have good answers for any of these questions, nor have we devoted sufficient attention to them. Much more than the physical properties of solar hardware, the institutional barriers and peculiarities of the market will determine what, where, when, who and how much, with regard to renewable sources.

Interestingly enough, solar energy, unlike most conventional energy sources, fits the economists' definition of a "public good." That is, solar energy is readily and universally available, can be shared by all, and one person's use does not diminish the capacity of other consumers to use and enjoy the resource. Despite its "public" character in the economic sense, solar is not being developed and marketed as a "public" good. This phenomenon could well truncate some of the most cost-effective markets for solar, and runs the very real risk of creating "solar chic" -- relegating solar to the role of a novelty for the affluent.

2. <u>Renewables Are A "Pivotal" Technology</u>

Renewable resources are not merely another new appliance to be grafted on to the industrialized way of life. Like many of the energy technologies which emerged before renewables, such as coal, natural gas or oil, solar is a pivotal technology which will fundamentally mold the infrastructure and environment of societies which deploy it. Renewable technologies will dramatically affect spacial form, population and industrial location, densities, social fabric and the quality of life itself. In essence, renewable technologies will be an arbiter of the sustaining and dynamic social and physical flows in our environment.

By analogy, the development of the automobile at the beginning of this century offers an interesting case in point. At the turn of the century there was relatively good, inexpensive, but crowded mass transit in urban areas. With mass production and use of the automobile, commentators asked what would happen to those who could not afford to purchase and operate this new miracle technology. The reply came that the automobile would be the savior for city life and mass transit. After all, wouldn't urban mass transit be less congested as the more affluent left subways for automobiles? Many years later, we can now see that far from improving mass transit, the automobile led to declining quality, more expensive transit, accompanied by suburban sprawl, segregation and environmental externalities which were not then foreseen.

I hope to convince you that for renewables the present situation is analogous with regard to the potential impact on those who are not able, because of the means by which we market renewable technologies, to share in this transition. The importance in terms of equity and socio-economic impact of the transition to renewables cannot be understated. It is probably the final transition in energy technology which this society will undertake. It is absolutely imperative that we learn from past errors to guide this transition in positive and equitable fashion.

Moreover, renewables are particularly pivotal with regard to urban areas. With solar, unlike many energy technologies, land <u>is</u> energy. Therefore, renewables will have different applications and impacts on built rather than new environments, and on dense rather than sprawled spacial forms. Traditionally, the cities have been importers of power. Decentralized resources offer the potential and the challenge to creatively change this equation. Our sensitivity to these facts as we manage the renewable transition will have dramatic impact on the viability of urban regions, especially older cities and the many elderly and disadvantaged which they harbor.

3. <u>Renewable Technologies Are Being Developed and Deployed In A Manner Which Is Barrier Blind</u>

We have been slow to address the many barriers which will inhibit, on a selective basis, the equitable use of solar power. Those barriers which we have initially addressed -- solar access, patent policy, utility rates for back-up power -- are primarily legal issues. And while I would not want to be accused of denying my brethren lawyers a new area of business, I believe that the toughest problems still lie in the institutional barriers which we have yet to address, including patterns of ownership, metering policy for multifamily units, growth policy, scale of renewable development, credit practices, and effective consumer access to and protection with these new technologies. These less visible barriers will shape our energy system and our childrens' world every bit as much as the technological components of these new technologies. These barriers, and their circumvention, must be an integral part of federal and state solar policies.

4. A Good Solar Policy Must Also Be A Good Urban And Social Policy

Opinion surveys indicate that the public views solar energy as one of the few positive and uplifting aspects of life as we enter the 1980's. However, solar hardware or design by itself is neither inherently good nor bad. We often think of a good solar policy as one which most quickly commercializes and deploys renewable technologies. Yet a vigorous solar commercialization policy is not necessarily a good urban policy, a good housing policy or a good social policy. In my opinion, the existing solar policy does not receive particularly high marks on any of these criteria, including its value as a commercialization strategy.

If we are to meet President Carter's goal of achieving 20% of our year 2000 energy budget with renewable resources, we will have to rely heavily on active systems. The Department of Energy has estimated that to achieve 2 quads of active solar heating and cooling by the year 2000 (to meet the Carter goal) we will have to construct 25 - 40 million new and retrofit systems within the next 20 years. If active systems do not meet our expectations, we will need even more installations to meet our goal. This cannot be accomplished if large segments of the market are screened off from effective participation by institutional barriers, as is now the case. If we are to achieve 40 million additional active heating and cooling units as a commercialization goal, we must deploy solar everywhere it makes economic sense, and not be restricted only to those homeowners who can afford significant front-end solar expenditures.

In this context, I would submit that over the next 20 years, the solar commercialization goal and the equity goal are identical. Without significant participation by all groups in all regions, the Carter's solar goal cannot be met. Moreover, only if we consciously plan the subsidization of solar to transcend the many institutional barriers which inhibit participation by a majority of our citizenry, can the truly remarkable potential of renewables to build a better world be fully realized. Absent this broader direction, we are bound to frustrate the realization of our housing and social goals.

Now that I have ground and sharpened along these four axes the lens through which I want us to view the impacts of renewable technologies, let me trace the repercussions of existing solar policies on our people and our regions. Specifically I want to focus on the impact of these policies on the future of our urban environments and their residents.

EXISTING SOLAR INITIATIVES

> Our guiding principle, as we developed this plan, was that above all it must be fair. None of our people must make an unfair sacrifice. None should reap an unfair benefit. The desire for equity is reflected throughout our plan.
>
> *President Jimmy Carter*
> *April 30, 1977*

With a few exceptions, the primary mechanisms chosen by the Carter Administration to stimulate the residential/commercial solar markets were tax credits and subsidized loans. The Energy Tax Act of 1978 includes a solar loan program (for which no funds have yet been appropriated). The Tax Act also features a non-refundable income tax credit equal to thirty percent of the first $2,000 and 20 percent of the next $8,000 (maximum $2,200 credit) spent on solar equipment. Within limits, the more income a family earned the higher the tax credit it could receive. For example, even spreading the credit over the allowed two years, a typical family of four earning less than the median family income of $16,000 per year would not be able to receive the full solar credit on an expenditure of the maximum $10,000.

A HUD consultant, the RUPI organization, has calculated that this tax credit would be <u>unavailable in full to 78 percent of American</u> taxpayers, and 65 percent of all present homeowners, because of insufficient liability to offset the full credit.[1] Moreover, these tax credits will allow less than 5 percent of program participants to be families with incomes under $16,000 per year (median family income).[2] As Table 1 illustrates, the great bulk of solar installations motivated by a tax credit would flow to those in the above $16,000 per year income brackets. The effects of such a credit are harshly regressive.

Table 1. Estimated distribution of homeowners installing solar hot water and space heating systems by income, under various incentives (with and without federal tax credit), 1978-1982.

Income	Total U.S. Homeowners (average 1978–1982)		Solar Hot Water				Combined Space Heating/ Hot Water			
			Baseline		Units Induced 40/25 Credit*		Baseline		Units Induced 40/25 Credit*	
	Number	%	Number	%	Number	%	Number	%	Number	%
0–$16,000	19,131,100	39%	8,800	5%	4,800	4%	500	4%	300	3%
$16,000–32,000	18,305,400	37%	63,400	36%	48,400	41%	3,900	30%	4,100	35%
$32,000–48,000	8,664,300	17%	69,900	39%	43,400	37%	6,400	49%	5,200	44%
$48,000+	3,431,500	7%	36,600	20%	22,000	19%	2,300	18%	2,200	18%
TOTAL	49,532,300		177,700		118,500		13,100		11,700	

*40/25 = 40% of first $1,000 and 25% of the next $6,400 (maximum credit of $2,000).

Note: Columns may not add due to rounding.

Source: RUPI, Federal Incentives for Solar Homes, 1977 at III-22.

Loans programs also exhibit inequitable features. Traditionally, homeowners have tended to pay cash, rather than encumber themselves with loans, for home improvements. The proposed Solar Bank legislation would augment existing but unfunded authority in the 1978 Energy Tax Act to offer subsidized interest, long-term loans for solar energy systems. However, it is most economical to solarize new rather than existing dwellings. Since a substantial mortgage loan is required usually for a new home, the solar unit costs simply can be added to the new mortgage.

Table 2 compares the projected market penetrations of various types of solar loans. Given the deductability of loan interest payments for federal income tax purposes, loans will be more attractive to taxpayers (1) in higher income brackets and (2) who itemize deductions. This will tend to exclude the elderly on fixed incomes (of whom over half own their own residences), those in relatively moderate or low income brackets, and renters who do not itemize deductions. As a group, this is over half of all American consumers. Clearly, it is not sound energy policy to disadvantage such a large segment of those citizens who already are most ravaged by the costs and uncertainties of energy supply.

Further, the pattern of penetration of solar technologies is particularly ominous for this nation's urban centers. New construction can accommodate both active and passive solar energy systems at much less cost than retrofitting existing homes.[3] Therefore, a disproportionate number of the homeowners motivated by subsidized Solar Bank loans will be those undertaking new construction, which primarily occurs in suburban and not in already-built urban areas.[4] The cities and their residents will be disproportionately excluded from sharing in solar's beneficence, and thus left as the prime residential supporters for existing utility systems.

IMPACTS ON THE RENTAL MARKET

Characteristics

Nationwide, approximately two-thirds of the total 76 million housing units are owner-occupied.[5] However, in central cities, the rental stock consistently exceeds owner-occupied housing.[6] The urban single family housing stock by virtue of its age, also is less well insulated and weatherized than its suburban counterparts.[7] In many urban areas, single landlords or holding companies own a vast amount of urban residential rental property.

Table 2. Market impact of separate solar loans: solar domestic hot water systems. Estimates for units installed over five-year period, 1978-1982.

	Market Impact—Cumulative Units					
Loan Terms	Retrofit	Percent Increase	New Homes	Percent Increase	Total	Percent Increase
No incentive	118,000	—	59,000	—	178,000	—
7%, 10 years	135,000	14%	67,000	12%	202,000	14%
5%, 10 years	145,000	23	72,000	21	217,000	22
3%, 15 years	159,000	34	82,000	38	241,000	36
1%, 20 years	177,000	50	99,000	67	277,000	56

Source: RUPI, Federal Incentives for Solar Homes, 1977 at IV-4.

Many owners of multi-family property have a threshold of five years or less when assessing payback periods and the cost effectiveness of capital improvements to buildings.[8]

Physically, high-rise multi-family structures can face problems in using solar energy. Since the available roof area relative to building space to be heated is often relatively small, special problems arise. Table 3 illustrates the various categories of existing multi-family design by number of dwellings. Especially in urban areas, many of the multi-family structures with greater than twenty units are of high-rise design. However, careful design tradeoffs between usable collector space (roofs, yards, tops of parking structures) and storage capacity can overcome some of the multi-family solar limitations in dense areas.[9]

Yet despite the difficulties of adapting renewable technologies to the urban housing stock, the importance of this project can not be overestimated. Utility costs presently account for about half of all operating expenses in multi-family housing, having doubled in the last 6 years.[10] DOE estimates that rising utility expenses may cause as much as a 15 percent rise in the default rate on government insured mortgages. Containment of these energy costs is prerequisite to the maintenance of healthy urban economies.

Metering

If the owner of multi-family housing does not pay utility bills there is scant incentive to make capital improvements for energy conservation. Without the constant monthly charge for utilities, there is no real financial benefit (aside from perhaps higher resale value) from undertaking gratuitous solar improvements. In that volume of the multi-family rental stock in which master meters make owners liable for utility bills,[11] owners still have an incentive to make solar and energy conservation improvements.

However, there has been a trend in the last few years to convert master utility metered rental dwellings to individual retail metering, in which tenants are directly responsible to utility companies for total energy consumption of their dwellings. If such metering conversion is undertaken prior to cost-effective energy conservation or solar improvements, the incentive for these improvements is permanently lost. Tenants have no legal ability or economic motivation for making such improvements.

Federal programs currently promote the conversion of metering in multi-family housing. A provision of the

Table 3. Total occupied housing units, 1975, by tenure and type of structure (rental only)

	Number of Units (in thousands)	Percent of Total Units	Percent of Rental Units
Renter Occupied Housing Units			
Size of Structure			
Mobile home	519	0.7%	2.0%
Detached 1 unit	7,082	9.8	27.6
Attached 1 unit	1,350	1.9	5.3
Total 1 Unit	8,951	12.4	34.9
2-4 units	6,772	9.4	26.4
5-9 units	3,028	4.2	11.8
10-19 units	2,514	3.5	9.8
20-49 units	2,058	2.8	8.0
50 or more	2,332	3.2	9.1
Total	25,656	35.4	100.0
Units by Tenure			
Total Renter-Occupied Housing Units	25,656	35.4%	100.0%
Owner-Occupied Housing Units	46,867	64.6	
Total Occupied Housing Units	72,523	100.0	

Source: RUPI, Federal Incentives for Solar Homes, 1977 at VII-4.

National Energy Conservation Policy Act makes available at the discretion of the Secretary of HUD, $2 billion of subsidized "conservation loans," which can be employed by landlords to switch utility metering from landlords to tenants.[12] Thus, under this federal incentive it will become as economic for landlords to shift the utility burden onto tenants as to shift the burden onto the sun. Moreover, it directly frustrates any attempt to accelerate the use of solar energy for residential purposes.

For several years, HUD has also encouraged conversion to individual retail metering in locally-owned public housing and subsidized housing. Since 1976 by regulation,[13] HUD has established conversion to retail or checkmeters as the <u>only absolute obligation for the use of</u> Modernization funds. This policy may be revised in the near future.[14] For public housing tenants the impact is doubly detrimental, since not only is the public housing stock uninsulated across the country, but public housing tenants are supplied grossly inefficient appliances by the housing authorities.[15] For reasons which have to do with the nature of multi-family residential ownership and the option of individual metering, which is directly competitive with solar improvements, it is highly unlikely that the existing federal solar program will exert any substantial impact on the rental market.

PHYSICAL LIMITATIONS IN THE URBAN ENVIRONMENT

There have been few comprehensive assessments as to the percentage of land in the urban environment that is available for solar collection. Several factors favorably influence the adaptability of urban solar energy systems. In densely built cities, there is a high ratio of building surface (for collectors) to open land. Additionally, many of the buildings in urban environments have flat roofs as opposed to the typical suburban slope roof; providing excellent opportunities to orient, and at the same time hide from view, solar collectors.[16] Furthermore, at the height of most urban rooftops there is little foliage to obstruct direct solar access. All of these factors make the urban environment adaptable for solar technologies.

On the other hand, the height of buildings in the urban environment often casts shadows which obstruct direct solar access for other buildings.[17] This in turn renders solar technology less adaptable to the urban environment. The extent to which these positive and negative factors interact will be site-specific within any area and thus not meaningfully subject to generalization. Hohenemser estimates that

Table 4. Residential property tax rates in selected large cities: 1974.

City	Effective Tax Rate per $100	
	Rank	Rate
Boston	1	$5.94
Buffalo	2	4.31
Milwaukee	3	3.63
Los Angeles	4	3.43
San Antonio	5	3.43
Indianapolis	6	3.29
Baltimore	7	3.24
Pittsburgh	8	2.82
Philadelphia	9	2.80
Chicago	10	2.75
Detroit	11	2.73
Dallas	12	2.60
Houston	13	2.38
Atlanta	14	2.24
San Diego	15	2.23
New York City	16	2.18
San Francisco	17	2.13
Cleveland	18	1.88*
Seattle	19	1.82
St. Louis	20	1.80
Memphis	21	1.77
Denver	22	1.71
Jacksonville	23	1.69
New Orleans	24	1.69
Kansas City	25	1.57
Phoenix	26	1.55
Washington, D.C.	27	1.54
Nashville	28	1.39
Cincinnati	29	1.31
Columbus	30	1.17

*OTA baseline assumption $200.

Source: Government of the District of Columbia, Department of Finance and Revenue, Tax Burdens in Washington, D.C. Compared with Major State and Local Tax Burdens in the Nation's Thirty Largest Cities (1974).

it would require one-third to one-sixth of the entire urban land mass to meet urban energy needs with solar power.[18]

However, when solar technology is viewed as a community resource, the economics and feasibility of urban solar become much more promising. Instead of each individual dwelling or building having to have sufficient solar access and storage capacity to meet its own needs, community based systems provide more flexibility. For example, San Francisco, the most densely populated city in California, and one of the most densely populated cities in the country, exhibits a density of twenty five persons per acre (or one thousand persons per 40 acres). To meet the residential solar heating needs of these one thousand persons, approximately 8 to 13 percent of the land area they residentially inhabit would need to be devoted to rooftop solar collectors.[19] Given the total building roof-top area plus covered parking structures and other surfaces suitable for solar collectors, this is not <u>per se</u> an excessive demand on urban land.[20]

URBAN TAX POLICIES

Unless specific exemptions are enacted for solar improvements, addition of a solar device could significantly contribute to yearly property tax bills. Tax rates in many large older cities have become prohibitive. The Urban Institute found that between 1967-72, "growing cities managed to cut their effective tax rates by more than 25 percent... while the declining cities were obliged to raise their rates by nearly 25 percent."[21] Table 4 ranks effective residential property tax rates in the 30 largest cities. As can be seen, the effective tax rate in Boston, at almost $6.00 per $100.00 of assessed valuation, is one-third higher than any other city surveyed. Eight of the ten cities with the highest effective tax rates are located in the northeast and Midwest regions of the country, where utility costs already are the highest in the nation.

On a $10,000 investment for a combined space/water solar heating system, a taxpayer in Boston would pay almost $600 each year in additional taxes, while a similar taxpayer in Los Angeles would pay $343 and a taxpayer in New York City would pay $218. For many middle income consumers, these additional costs would make solar improvements unattractive and unaffordable. It has been estimated that property taxes alone can add as much as 10-25% to the cost of using solar energy[22] and reduce the value of annual savings by as much as 20-70%.[23] Obviously, the federal government cannot directly exempt solar devices from local property taxation. However, as part of its comprehensive solar program the federal government could offset lost local property tax revenues from solar abatements.

INSTITUTIONAL PRACTICES OF LENDERS

Private lending institutions will be the conduits to finance the transition to solar energy. To date, lending institutions have shown little interest in underwriting solar energy. In California, often considered the solar vanguard, less than 10 percent of the state's banks, savings and loan associations or credit unions offered special solar or conservation loan programs, according to a recent survey.

Banks and other lending institutions are understandably reluctant to offer mortgages for residential buildings which employ what is considered exotic energy technology. In a recent survey, 63 percent of lending institutions interviewed reported that they would "exclude the excess cost (of solar equipment) from the appraised value of the house" in determining the range of money they would loan.[24] An additional 22 percent of lenders interviewed indicated that they would lower the loan-to-value ratio of any loan they contemplated on a residence including solar technology.[25]

The inability to obtain sufficient financing for solar devices at reasonable rates may be particularly aggravated in urban areas. With urban populations many lending institutions have adopted strict definition of "credit-worthiness." In addition, de facto red-lining practices have steered mortgage money away from credit-worthy borrowers merely because of the geographic location of their properties.[26] Moreover, Richard Morris documents that banks, following the lead of the federal government, withdrew from lending in older American cities in 1973, two years before there was any basis for concluding that cities were in trouble:

> In 1975 Washington channeled 29 percent of its loan insurance to three states - Florida, California and Arizona - which had, together, 15 percent of the country's population. By insuring loans in the Sunbelt and not in the Northeast, Washington led the way for the bank red-lining of American Cities.[27]

To reiterate our third axiom, solar now is being deployed in a manner which is blind to these barriers. Oftentimes, rental projects are expected to be self-sustaining and to generate enough cash flow to make necessary improvements without major additional infusions of equity capital. When extra cash is generated from rental property, it must compete against other investments which the owner might make.

Additionally, multi-family structures are often built with a goal of reducing cost per unit. In 1976, the average cost of new rental housing built was less than half the cost of new owner occupied housing.[28]

BEGGARING THE CITIES

Totally aside from individual equity considerations, the inherent focus of solar subsidies could be a disaster for besieged urban areas. Urban areas harbor large numbers of those least likely to benefit from existing solar programs -- the poor, elderly and renters. In excluding these groups of the population from sharing in solar's beneficence, we will be curtaining off our urban centers from more competitive renewable energy systems. From the perspective of the fourth axis, a careless solar policy could be a disastrous urban and social policy.

Nationally, about 26 million of a total 76 million dwelling units (34 percent) are rented year round.[29] However, this 34 percent of rental dwellings is not spread uniformly between cities and suburbs. In large Eastern cities, the population of rental housing dwarfs that in surrounding suburbs. 71 percent of New York's 1.8 million occupied housing units are rented. In Boston, 73 percent of the housing stock is rented.[30] The suburbs surrounding these two central cities have a majority of owner occupied housing.

In sharp contrast, in many of the newest cities, the proportion of rental housing is just slightly above the national average. In Seattle, only 41 percent of the housing stock is rented;[31] and in metropolitan Phoenix, 37 percent of the 365,000 housing units are rented.[32] This means that the unavailability of solar for the cities will be two-fold: First, solar technology will be focused on the suburbs to the exclusion of urban areas, and second, older urban areas with a high proportion of rental stock will be relatively disadvantaged compared to newer cities with a lesser amount of rental stock. It should also be noted that many of the newer cities do not experience the same physical constraints as some of the more densely urbanized and landlocked older cities. As presently enacted, national solar initiatives could make energy islands of the older urban areas.

NEGATIVE IMPACTS UPON PRICES OF CONVENTIONAL UTILITY SERVICES FOR URBAN RESIDENTS

Utilities do not serve geographic regions which correspond to political subdivisions. Large investor-owned utilities usually have a service area which includes urban, suburban and often rural customers served from the same

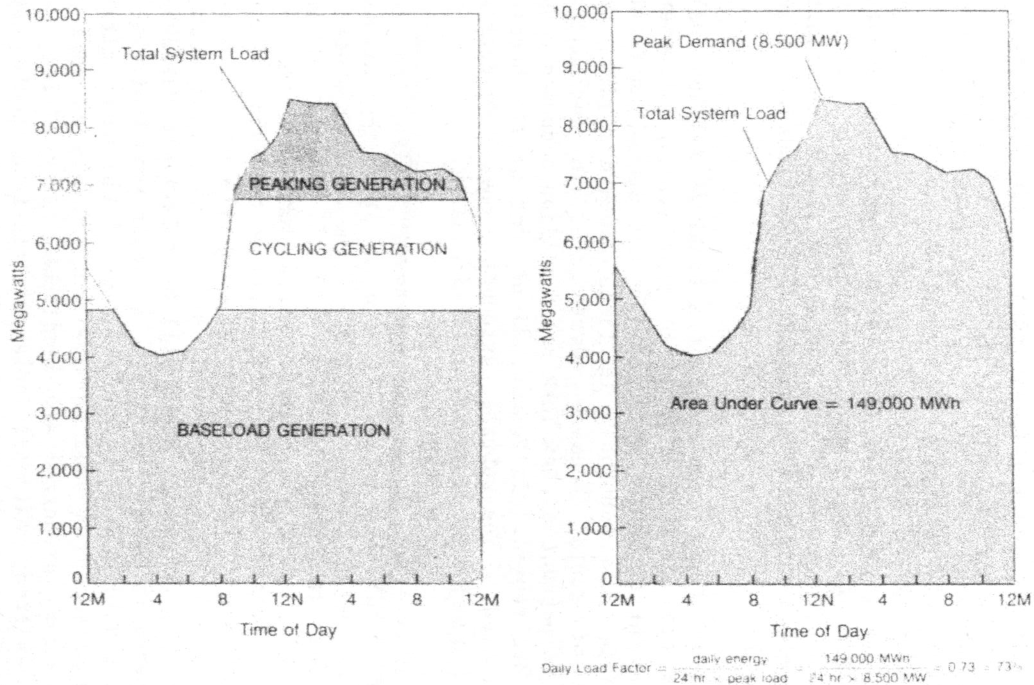

Figure 1. Dispatching generation to meet a cyclical load. Reprinted by permission from Rate Design and Load Control (Palo Alto, Calif.: Electric Power Research Institute, 1977).

network of generating facilities. Power sharing and pooling arrangements often extend the geographic reach of utility generating facilities beyond the immediate boundaries of a company's regulated service area. With the existing system of subsidies for conventional fossil and uranium fuels, utilities will continue to generate power for their service areas through expansion of conventional rather than solar alternatives.[33]

Since the cost of a 100 percent solar heating system does not greatly exceed the cost of a solar heating system capable of delivering 75 percent of heating needs,[34] many of those residences or commercial establishments which adopt solar energy may be able to largely, if not totally, generate their own heating energy. This, in effect, will allow many of these residences to effectively "disconnect" from their utility companies, except during particularly cold periods when their collectors and storage capacity are not sufficient to meet heating needs.

This phenomenon will alter the timing and magnitude of electricity sales. Unlike many commodities, electricity can not now be produced economically in advance and stored on the shelf until needed. Utilities must have sufficient installed generating facilities in order to be able to instantaneously meet whatever demand for electricity customers require at any moment. Figure 1 illustrates the daily load profile of a typical utility. To the degree that expensive generating facilities lie idle, tremendous inefficiency for the utility system results. Thus, the economics of producing electricity and the prices that consumers must pay, can vary greatly.

Loss of Seasonal Off-Peak Electric Load

There are two possible negative phenomena which could result if solar power is driven by federal policy to primarily suburban areas. These are an increase in daily peak electric demand or a loss of seasonal off peak electric load. The occurrence of these depends on exactly what type of solar technology is deployed under federal policies.

Most utility companies qualify as "summer peaking." That is, across an entire year, the maximum demand for electricity they experience occurs in the summer months — on those summer days when maximum use is made of air conditioning. Even for summer peaking utilities, there is usually a substantial demand during the coldest months of winter when electric resistance heating customers make maximum demand upon the system. Annually more than half of the new homes constructed in the country use electric heating, and their percentage is increasing yearly.[35]

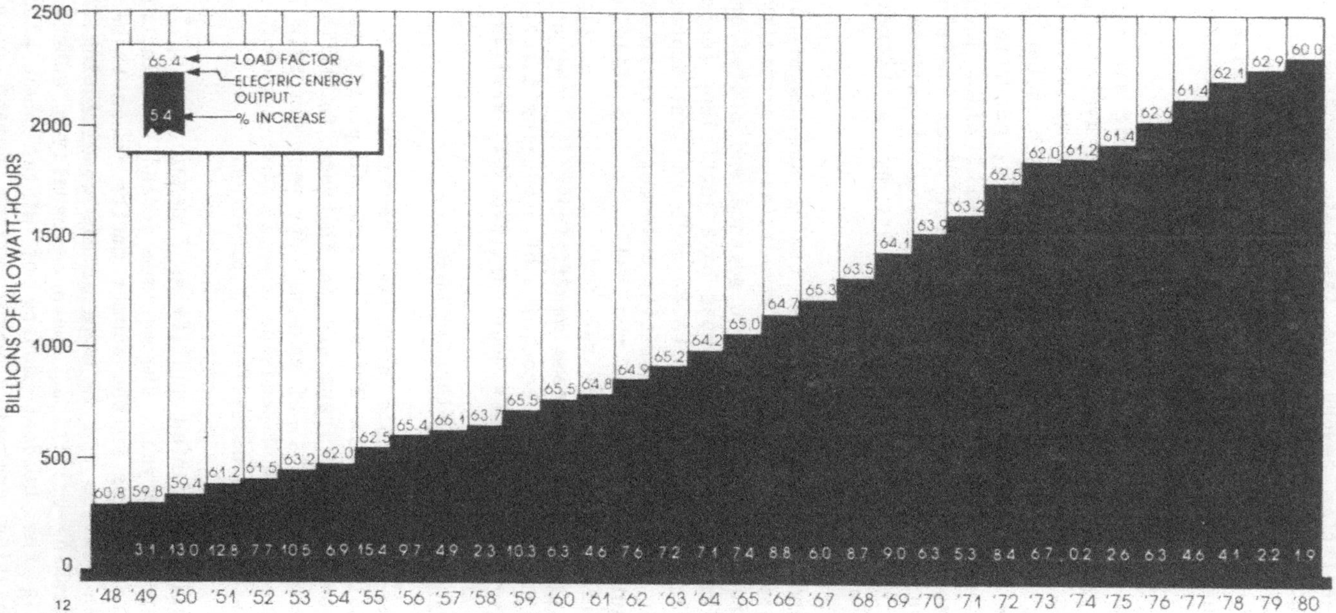

Figure 2. Electric energy output and annual load factors—total electric utility industry of the contiguous United States. Reprinted by permission from 1980 Year-End Electric Power Survey (Washington, D.C.: Edison Electric Institute, 1981; pub. no. 04-81-04).

To the degree that solar heating displaces new or existing electric heating it will diminish the volume of electricity sales during the winter season. Summer peaking utilities will have to maintain an undiminished capacity to meet summer demand, while winter sales are reduced as a result of solar heating. This is what utility executives refer to as a displacement of fuel without a corresponding displacement of capacity. Utilities will have to spread a huge fixed volume of capital costs (to build and maintain facilities) over a declining total volume of electricity sales. Therefore for each kilowatt/hour of electricity sold, customers will have to absorb a larger and larger share of the billions of dollars of fixed capital costs of a typical utility. Customers left dependent on traditional fossil-fueled supply will see their electricity costs increase irrespective of increases in fossil fuel prices. Utility consumers will be caught in a double bind: They will pay not only for rising fossil fuel costs but also for decreased efficiency of electric power systems.

These system inefficiencies are referred to as decreasing utility load factors. A load factor is simply the ratio of peak load to total generating capacity (including a reserve margin). The larger the load factor, the more the utility's capital is being used over the course of the year, and the more efficient is the utility generating system. The more efficient the system, the cheaper the price of electricity to customers, ceteris paribus.

Figure 2 illustrates historic U.S. system peak load and reserve margins. As can be seen from this diagram the aggregate reserve margin has been increasing each year since 1960. Similarly, Figure 3 illustrates the load factor for all electric utilities in the U.S. This chart similarly demonstrates that since about 1960, the load factor (efficiency) of the U.S. electric system has been decreasing. To the extent that solar exacerbates seasonally poor load factors, traditional utility customers will have to pay more for power from an increasingly inefficient system. In contrast, those who make the transition to solar energy will be able to not only buffer themselves against the higher costs of fossil fuels, but largely avoid their share for this decreasing efficiency.

The impacts in certain highly urbanized areas could be devastating. Those industries, commercial establishments and relatively affluent homeowners able to afford a transition to solar energy will generate their own power. The U.S. Office of Technology Assessment has concluded that:

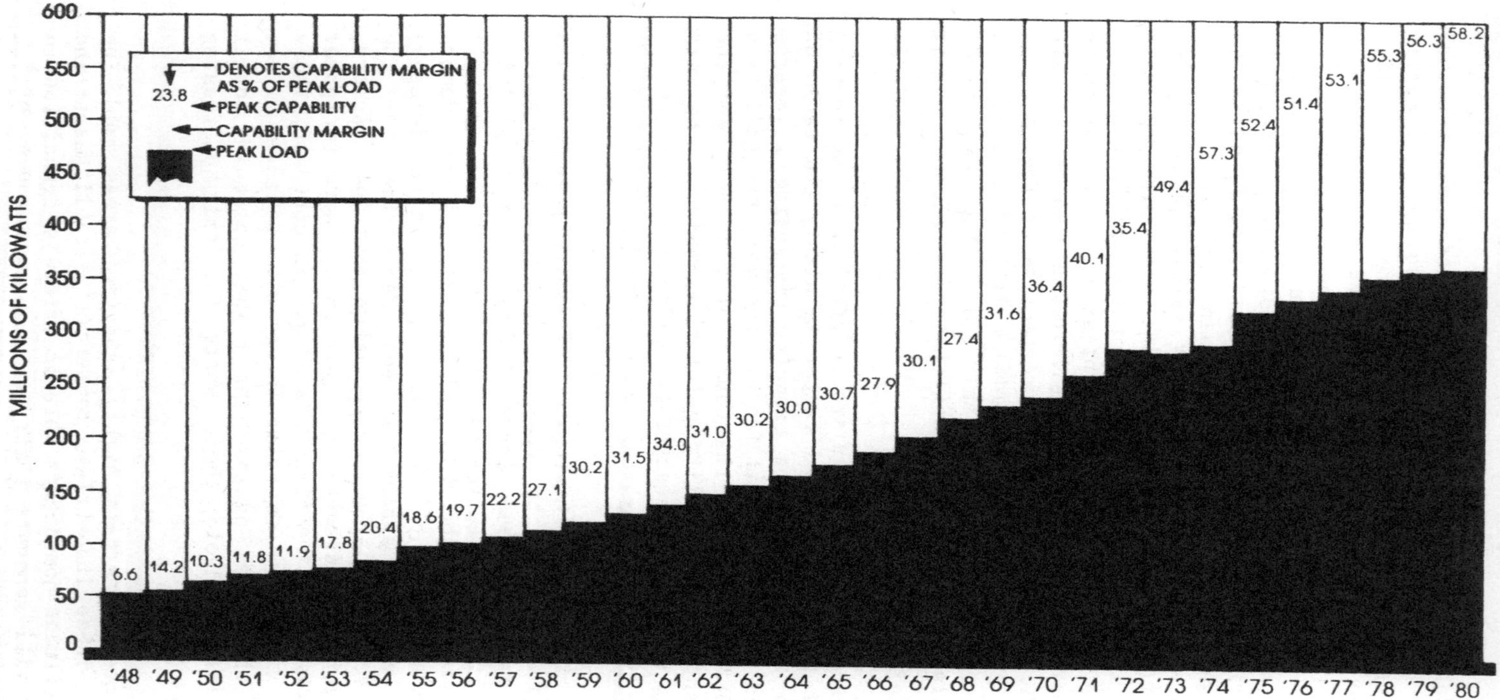

Figure 3. December peak capabilities, peak loads, and capability margins—total electric utility industry of the contiguous United States. Peak capability represents the maximum kilowatt output with all power sources available. Capability margin includes the provision for maintenance, emergency outages, and system operating requirements. Note: All values indicated are for December and do not reflect that maximum loads in some regions occur in summer. Reprinted by permission from _1980 Year-End Electric Power Survey_ (Washington, D.C.: Edison Electric Institute, 1981; pub. no. 04-81-04).

> Within 3-5 years it should be possible to construct systems capable of supplying all of the heating and hot water requirements of large buildings at prices which would be competitive with conventional electric heating...[36]

This phenomenon is already occuring in New York City using diesel power, with potentially dire consequences for Consolidated Edison, the largest and highest cost electric utility in the country. Since 1975, several dozen apartment complexes have started generating their own power. [37] In June of this year a major thirty-two story office building in mid-town Manhattan began undertaking a $26 million renovation project to entirely remove the building from the Con Ed system. A Con Ed official explained that the withdrawal of only one hundred buildings from the Con Ed system, could decrease demand by 5 percent and increase costs for all other consumers by 3 percent.[38]

The implications for urban areas are ominous. As the prices for utility service increases as fossil fuel prices increase and system efficiency declines, utilities face at least two options which will have undesirable impact upon non-solar urban consumers. First, they may seek to lower the rates charged for utility service to industries and commercial facilities in order to prevent mass exodus from the area or a switch to self-generation. Consolidated Edison in New York City proposed doing precisely this.[39] If this occurs, these revenue deficiencies must be recouped from higher rates charged to residential customers. Second, utilities could allow the quality of their service to decline, further encouraging relocation and withdrawal from the system. In either of these events, the impact on the urban areas will be negative and regressive.

<u>Increase in Daily Peak Electric Demand</u>

Households which utilize solar technology for heating have a variety of sources available for backup heat; among these electric heating is most prominently mentioned by many experts.[40] Because the need for backup power for a solar heating system can occur on a cloudy winter day, as well as during sunless evening hours, the additional demand for this daytime backup power could increase daily peak electric load. This could result in the use of more expensive peaking generators to meet this demand, and conceivably could require utilities to build or at least accelerate the construction of additional peak generating capacity. The result would be higher electric costs for everyone, <u>ceteris paribus</u>.

Table 5. Components of Employment Change Between 1969 and 1974, in the North and South.

Region	Total Job Opportunities	Percent Change 1969–74	Change in Jobs as a Percent of 1969 Level, attributable to:				
			Closure of Firms	Birth of Firms	Expansion/ Contraction	Migration out of Region	Migration in to Region
North	20,718,094	-5.8	20.5	8.9	5.6	0.21	0.06
New England	2,897,583	-7.4	21.9	9.4	4.5	0.11	0.03
Middle Atlantic	8,731,946	-11.1	21.7	8.6	2.0	0.27	0.06
East North Central	9,088,565	-0.3	18.9	9.1	9.5	0.18	0.08
South	20,983,550	+11.6	21.7	17.1	15.7	0.16	0.61

Rates of Closure, Birth, In- and Outmigration of Firms in the North and South, 1969–1974

Region	Closure Rate	Birth Rate	Inmigration Rate	Outmigration Rate
North	0.33	0.20	0.0002	0.0007
New England	0.33	0.22	0.0022	0.0009
Middle Atlantic	0.33	0.18	0.0005	0.0017
East North Central	0.33	0.22	0.0005	0.0008
South	0.35	0.29	0.0010	0.0003

Source: C. Jusenius and L. Ledebur, Documenting the "Decline" of the North (1977).

A great number of variables will influence whether and to what degree solar power will increase daily peak demand, worsen utility load factors and raise costs. Chief among these are the electric load management capabilities of solar heating systems,[41] electric rate structures,[42] the generating mix and construction program of utilities, the prices of competing fuels and federal and state tax practices. Research under widely varying assumptions yields contradictory results -- finding that a partial shift to solar power will raise electric peak demand,[43] and to the contrary that it will not raise peak demand.[44]

I am convinced, after reviewing the literature, that to the extent to which generalizations can be made, the potential problem of solar adding to electric peak demand can be minimized with existing load management capabilities. The common practice of pricing all electricity sales at average cost across the day and seasons, irrespective of its costs of generation, coupled with discriminatory demand charges many electric utilities are assessing solar users for backup power, could well discourage the use of electricity as a primary backup energy source.

I believe the problem of loss of seasonal non-peak electric load resulting from conversion from electric to solar heat, previously discussed, poses a greater impact on electric load factors and customer costs.

INDUSTRIAL RELOCATION AND JOB IMPACTS

Energy is the fastest rising cost for most industrial and commercial establishments. Therefore one would expect that as energy prices and availability vary, industry would make its locational decisions accordingly. For example, the fact that Con Edison in New York charges $15,000 for a quantity of industrial electricity that costs about $7,500 in Chicago and $9,500 in Los Angeles, has an impact in locational decisions for any potentially mobile energy consuming corporation.[45]

To date, the growth in suburban and Sunbelt jobs has not been so much the product of relocation from Northeast and Midwest urban areas, as the location of most new companies in the former regions.[46] Nonetheless, the growth rates of employment in urban areas in the Northeast and North Central regions were much less than the growth rates of their respective metropolitan regions, which in turn were much less than growth rates in the booming South and West.[47] This phenomenon is clearly illustrated by Table 5. Since 1960, the Northeast has lost almost a million manufacturing jobs, while the South has gained 1.5 million.[48] Central city manufacturing jobs in the frostbelt have decreased even more radically than those in the frostbelt as a whole.[49]

With the transition to solar energy a new wrinkle will be added to industrial location decisions. There are two likely locational pressures which will result from the deployment of industrial solar technologies: (1) a relocation to the sunnier (Sunbelt) regions of the country where solar insolation is maximum, and (2) a relocation to suburban areas to take advantage of greater space for solar collector devices and possibly lower backup utility rates (depending upon whether a different utility company serves the suburbs than serves the urban area). Either of these pressures may cause an exodus of industry from the cities, undercutting the urban economic and tax bases. There is ample evidence that this pressure is already occuring.[50]

REALIGNMENT OF POLICY

It is vitally important for several reasons that solar technologies be realistically available to and utilized by all segments of society. First, precisely because solar is a pivotal energy technology which will dramatically alter land-use, economic and social relationships, it is essential that solar technologies be implemented in a manner which promotes equity and strengthens all geographic regions. Second, U.S. Department of Energy analysis indicates that the largest potential for active systems is in multifamily design. It is important that there be developed a body of knowledge and experience for installing solar in multifamily structures, which pose some of the most interesting problems and offer some of the greatest promise for solar technologies.

Third, if the country is entering a crash program to eliminate reliance upon foreign oil, we would be suffering from sun stroke to not vigorously exploit, in all regions and buildings, the cost-effective potential available now from decentralized renewable resources. Indeed, it may be the only means by which to achieve energy independence. Solar can be the ideal counter-cyclical, anti-inflationary, job-creating federal program to promote economic well being if the program is correctly designed.

To accomplish this realignment of policy, one must design solar policy while looking through the lens we fashioned at the outset of this discourse. First, because renewables are a pivotal technology, their development and deployment must be carefully planned so as to ensure equitable impacts.

Because, unlike gas and electric utilities, solar will be provided by a decentralized non-monopoly industry, consumer assurance becomes crucially important in the delivery of solar technologies. Second, since solar is a "public good," it should be developed and marketed at least in part on a community or district basis. This will involve not only rethinking the mix of solar hardware, but also realigning our subsidy programs and our delivery mechanisms. The mechanisms need to demonstrate the desirability of community-scale solar to large numbers of urban dwellers, renters and low income persons able to share in the solar transition.

Third, the subsidization and marketing of renewable technologies must be tailored to the institutional and legal barriers which exist. It is much easier to change a few federal and state subsidy programs than it is to alter thousands of building codes, the distribution of income and 300 years of ownership patterns. Fourth, solar commercialization policy must be developed in a manner complementary to national housing, economic development and social goals. Moreover, solar policy must parallel a sensible urban, as well as suburban, agenda.

There are some promising signs. Congressman Henry Reuss has included in the House of Representatives' version of the Solar and Conservation Bank Bill two key provisions. The first would include other than single family owners in the eligibility for subsidized solar loans. Urban and rural coops, neighborhood associations and tenant groups would be eligible to pool their subsidies to collectively utilize renewable technologies. They would also receive technical assistance in bringing a project to fruition. Second, low income persons would be eligible for a subsidy of up to 60% of a system's cost (a 50% larger subsidy than generally provided under the legislation).

While these provisions would only open a window to renewables for individuals and groups who would otherwise have no practical access to these technologies, they do not guarantee the equitable deployment of solar resources. But they are a very important start. My colleagues and I are working on a variety of other mechanisms to achieve consumer assurance, to begin to reach the existing multifamily housing stock and to bring solar into publicly assisted housing. Out of our common concern, I believe, can come the dawning of a sustainable and more just world.

REFERENCES

1. RUPI, Federal Incentives for Solar Homes: An Assessment of Program Options, 1977.

2. Ibid, at III-6.

3. Ibid. at IV-12, 13.

4. Inner-city housing construction is proceeding at only half the pace of metropolitan housing starts; See HUD, The President's National Urban Policy Report, 1978 at 59.

5. HUD, Statistical Yearbook, 1976 at 261.

6. Urban Policy Report, supra note 5 at 59.

7. Ibid.

8. Therefore, a $2,000 solar hot water system or a $10,000 combined water/space heating system would comprise a much higher fraction of the cost of a new rental unit than a new owner-occupied unit. To date it is estimated that only 4 percent of total residential solar installations have been in multi-family rental housing.

9. See generally, LBL, supra note 1 at Chapter XI.

10. Institute of Real Estate Management, Income and Expense Analysis: Apartments, Condominiums and Cooperations, 1978.

11. While the exact number of master metered multi-family units is unknown, HUD estimates that over 70 percent of public housing is currently master metered. Draft Minutes of February 27, 1978. Meeting of HUD Task Force on Tenant Participation in the Management of Low Income Housing (Statement of Kenneth Moul) at 5. About half of all multi-family housing (about 12 million units) is master metered for heating. U.S. Dept. of Energy, Alternative Metering Practices, HCP/M 1693-03, June 1979.

12. Section 243 of Pub. L. 95-619(1978).

13. 24 C.F.R. §§ 865.404 et seq.

14. See proposed HUD conservation regulation, 43 Fed. Reg. 60854 et seq (Dec. 28, 1978).

15. 41 C.F.R. §§ 1-1.301, ,cu et seq.

16. 500 Professional Builder, June 1976 at 105.

17. New York State Legislative Commission on Energy Systems, Forum on Solar Access, July, 28, 1977, at 8-18.

18. Kurt Hohenesmer, "Energy Efficiency Versus Energy Growth," in Environment, July 1978 at 5.

19. Given present technology, 50,000 to 80,000 ft. of collector surface would be required. This would consume three to five acres of roof-top surface or other urban land with good solar exposure. Three to five acres out of a gross acreage of 40 acres, attributable to one thousand residents living at a density of twenty five persons per acre, must be used for solar collectors.

20. See, Lawrence Berkeley Laboratory, Distributed Energy Systems in California's Future, Vol. 1 at 103-105.

21. Urban Policy Report, supra, note 5 at 78.

22. U.S. Office of Technology Assessment, Application of Solar Technology to Today's Energy Needs, 1978 at 78.

23. RUPI, supra note 2 at VI-23.

24. RUPI, Home Mortgage Lending and Solar Energy, 1977 at 13.

25. Id. at 99.

26. National Housing and Economic Development Law Project, Red-lining and Disinvestment: Causes Consequences and Proposed Remedies, prepared for HUD Hearings on July 14-16, 1976. Red-lining can take the form of outright refusal to invest in a neighborhood, requiring higher down payments, higher loan interest rates, higher loan closing costs, shorter loan maturities, appraisal of property for loan purposes below the actual market value and charging excessive discount "points."

27. Richard S. Morris, Bum Rap On America's Cities: The Real Causes of Urban Decay, 1978 at 12, 13.

28. R.S. Means Co., Building Construction Cost Data, 1976.

29. HUD Statistical Yearbook, 1976 at 261 (as updated).

30. Steven Ferrey, personal conversation with local government officials in New York City and Boston.

31. Steven Ferrey, conversation with Seattle HUD office.

32. Steven Ferrey, conversation with Phoenix HUD office, which relied on the newspaper publication "Inside Phoenix."

33. Duane Chapman, Taxation and Solar Energy, Solar Energy Office, California Energy Commission (1978).

34. OTA Study, supra note 24 at 42.

35. Letter to Steven Ferrey from Walter Maczka, Electric Light and Power Magazine, August 5, 1977. Almost one million homes built during 1976 were heated electrically.

36. OTA Study, supra note 24 at 18.

37. Environmental Action Foundation, Power Line, July 1978, at 3.

38. Energy Users News, supra note 50.

39. Energy Users News, May 29, 1978 at 6.

40. In new construction electric heating eliminates the need to install a furnace. Either electric resistance or electric heat pump technology can be employed.

41. Electric Load Management is the use of electricity at night to charge solar heat storage tanks, thus shifting the demand for backup power to off peak times. Load managed electric backup has the advantage of using off peak baseload or intermediate load electric power, increasing load factors and placing no pressure on the utility to expand capacity. However, given the variable nature of solar insolation, it is extremely difficult for most homeowners to anticipate the night before how much night time electric heat they should store to augment the next day's potential sunshine. The ability to successfully load manage the use of electric backup heat is thus dramatically limited by the inability to predict accurately the weather. See generally, Daviton, Bright & Marcuse, Utility Load Management and Solar Energy, Brookhaven National Laboratory, 1979.

42. Marginal cost pricing would promote the use of off-peak electric backup for solar power.

43. See Nathanson, et al, System Definition Study, Phase I of Individual Load Center, Solar Heating and Cooling Residential Project, EPRI, ER-594, 1977; Feldman and Anderson, Utility Pricing and Solar Energy, Clark University, 1976; Asbury and Mueller, "Solar Energy Electric Utilities: Should They Be Interfaced", in Science, 195, February 4, 1977.

44. Critcher and Milton, Solar Heating and Cooling of Buildings: Requirements Definition and Impact Analysis, EPRI, ER-808-54, 1978; Davitian, Bright and Marcuse, op. cit.

45. Energy Users News, July 17, 1978 at 15.

46. Dun and Bradstreet calculates that only 3 percent of the job losses in the Middle Atlantic states since 1960 are the direct result of relocation to the Sunbelt.

47. Ibid. at 26

48. Ibid. at 20.

49. Ibid. at 35.

50. Ashmont Systems, Inc. is now considering locating a steel mill in the former Brooklyn Navy Yard's industrial park. This mill would employ 1,500 to 2,000 workers, 80 percent of whom would be minorities. However, the project is not economically viable if the mill would have to purchase Con Edison's exorbitantly priced electricity. If the Navy Yard cogenerates its own power, Con Edison would lose one of its 20 largest customers. The strange paradox results that to attract jobs, the load factors of the utility must decrease and the costs to other customers increase. Energy Users News, October 2, 1978 at 1, 8.

Part 4

International Perspective

Måns Lönnroth, Thomas B. Johansson, Peter Steen

6. Sweden Beyond Oil: Nuclear Commitments and Solar Options

SUMMARY

The project "Energy and Society", sponsored by the Swedish Secretariat for Futures Studies, has studied different indigenous alternatives to imported oil in Sweden. One alternative is nuclear energy, another is renewable energy. Large uncertainties are associated with both alternatives today. The main characteristics of an energy policy for the rest of the century that does not foreclose either of these options have been identified. Such a policy will have to be based on an understanding of similarities and differences between the alternatives.*

A nuclear and a solar energy system has been outlined as a basis for an analysis of technical, economical and institutional issues.

Having no domestic oil, gas or coal, Sweden is 70% dependent on imported oil. This will have to change, either due to resource depletion within the next several decades, or due to oil-rich countries limiting export.

Thus there has to be a transition, but to what? And what factors will shape the energy path of Sweden? It is necessary to look into what alternatives exist for replacing oil on a major scale.

Several decades are needed for major changes in the energy system to take place. Most energy policy studies are based on the need to assure supply in the short and medium

* Based on a book with the title Solar versus Nuclear: Choosing Energy Futures, published by Pergamon Press, Oxford, England, January 1980.

term. The longer term development thus tends to be determined more through an incremental series of short term decisions rather than as a result of any overall strategy or vision. Since we believe such an approach to be inherently inappropriate to these technologies, we have worked differently.

We have therefore identified two different long-term energy systems based on indigenous resources for Sweden. From these we have deduced the steps that are necessary in the short and medium term in order to make these longer term developments possible. One such system is based on indigenous uranium. Sweden has some 15% of the world's uranium reserves in low-grade shale deposits as yet unmined. The other system is based on renewable energy. Sweden enjoys a solar energy influx close to 1 MWh/m^2year on a horizontal surface.

The course of events until mid 1970s has clearly moved in the direction of large scale adaption of nuclear energy. Various decisions taken during 1955-1965 led to the establishment of a Swedish reactor industry during the 1960s and to a major nuclear investment program during the 1970s. By 1973, 11 reactors were licenced (8.4 GW) and the utilities planned for 25 GW by 1990. This would have made the Swedish nuclear program the largest in the world on a per capita basis. Since the mid-70s, nuclear energy has been the most important issue in Swedish politics, contributing to the bringing down of one government in 1976 and forcing one to resign in 1978. The political fall-out in Sweden from Three Mile Island included a decision to hold a referendum about the role of nuclear energy in 1980 (the first referendum in 20 years and the fourth during this century). Nevertheless, important groups (utilities, industry, some trade unions, etc.) argue that nuclear energy is the only realistic large scale alternative to imported oil in Sweden. Others hold that alternatives probably do exist and should not be discarded until they have been studied wih the same intensity as the nuclear alternative already has been. These views are backed by a relatively large, but dispersed, constituency including environmentalists, women's organizations, several youth organizations within political parties, etc.

However, there seem today to be major uncertainties with both the solar and the nuclear options: technically, environmentally, economically, institutionally and socially.

The Swedish society therefore has to start on a transitional path, but without having a clear consensus of where to go. Except for relatively small groups, who already have made up their minds about nuclear and solar energy, a fairly large majority on the Swedish political scene favor a strategy of preserving (and creating) freedom of action (1). Our work has been directed towards understanding the technical and economic characteristics and the political dynamics of such a strategy.

The starting point for the discussion has to be the characteristics of a nuclear and a solar energy system. We now proceed to discuss their technical and economic properties and potentials. Their similarities and differences, together with their social and institutional implications, constitute the lead theme of our study.

ASSUMPTIONS ON ENERGY DEMAND

Some basic data on Sweden are given in Table 1.

We have chosen for the year 2015 a model of a Swedish society with roughly the same societal and industrial structure as today. The number of inhabitants is assumed to remain at about 8 million. The production of goods and services in the country is assumed to be twice the level of today. It should be noted that the Swedish level is already one of the highest in the world and, compared to the U.S., for example, Sweden is also rather energy efficient (2). The level of production assumed (Table 2) would permit giving everyone about the material standard now enjoyed by the top 10 percent of the population.

Other mixes of goods and services are, of course, rather likely but do not greatly affect the gross features of the energy system. The assumptions therefore cover different developments of the Swedish society; they even include more emphasis on conservation of resources than it was necessary to assume, as well as a general raising of the standard of living.

With the sketched outline of economic activity, the final demand of energy is that shown in Table 2. The assumptions of specific energy use must be regarded as conservative.

Figure 1 relates this demand to current Swedish energy policy.

A breakdown of the energy use in Sweden into several energy quality groups has been done for the energy demand of 1971. The same distribution is assumed for 2015, although a small adjustment has been made for increased efficiency in space heating. The resulting breakdown of energy quality is included in Figures 2 and 3.

Table 1. Some basic data for Sweden (1975). Electricity is traditionally counted as 1 kWh_{th} because of dominating hydro power production.

Area	450,000 km^2	Energy total	415 kWh/year
Population	8,200,000	Energy/capita	50 MWh/year
GNP	$52,000,000,000	Electricity	80 TWh/year
		Hydropower	57 TWh/year
		Nuclear	12 TWh/year

Table 2. Energy use in the year 2015, based on figures for 1975.

	1975 TWh	2015 TWh
Production of goods and services	165	264
Transportation	75	75
Other	70	70
Housing, including household electricity	80	80
Total	390	489
Conversion losses	25	58-79
Total Supply	415	547-568

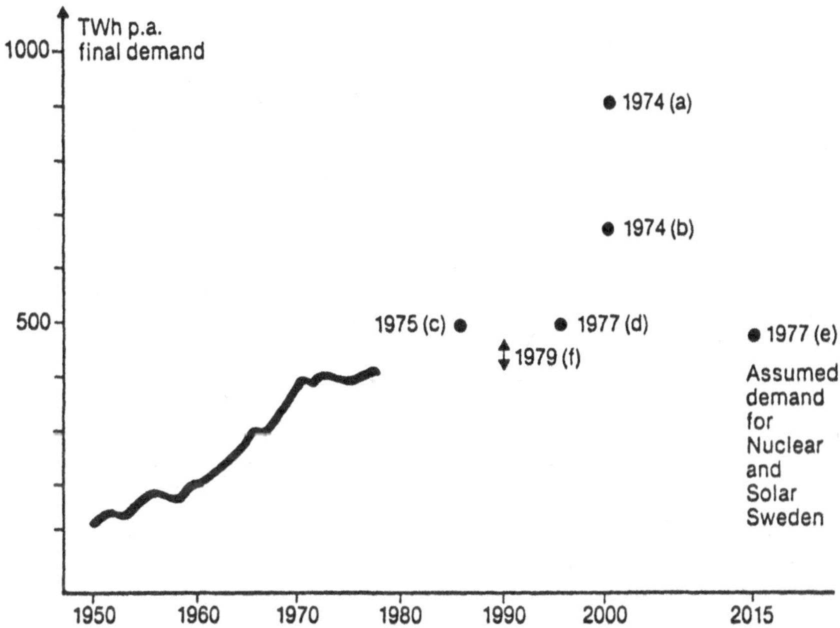

Figure 1. Energy demand up to 1978. The points mark various official demand estimates and clearly illustrate how projected levels of energy demand have been reduced during the last five years due to increased understanding of energy demand, lower economic growth, and conservation efforts. 1974 (a) is based on an assumption of 6 percent p.a. growth in industrial output; 1974 (b) is based on 4 percent p.a. growth; 1975 (c) is the government bill; 1977 (d) is a forecast made by the Swedish Board of Industries, based on 3.3 percent p.a. growth of industrial output; 1977 (e) is the figure used for Solar and Nuclear Sweden; 1979 (f) is the demand level assumed by the government bill of 1979.

NUCLEAR—SWEDEN

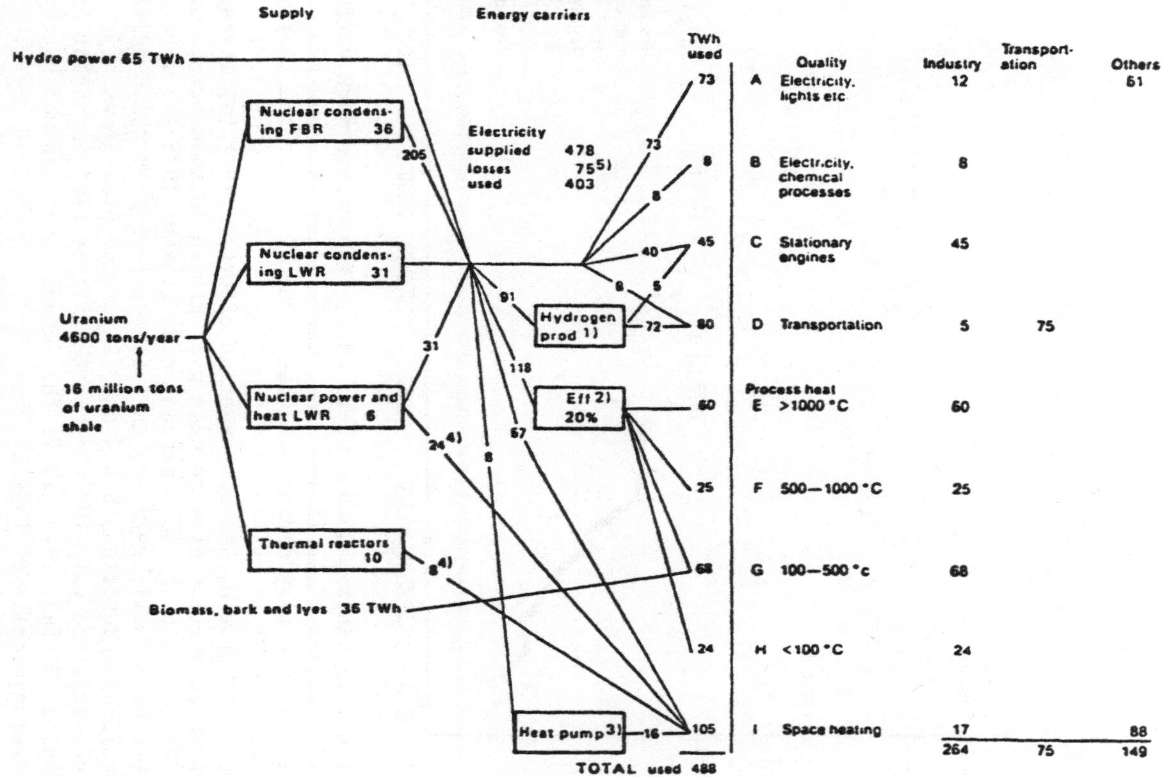

Figure 2. The energy system in Nuclear Sweden in 2015. The supply of energy in the system is shown on the left; on the right is illustrated the energy consumption divided into different categories A-I of energy quality. The linkage between supply and consumption is shown in the middle. The figures indicate the number of TWh represented by each line.

1) 85 percent efficiency, possibly methanol instead but also requires coal or wood.

2) Assumed 20 percent higher efficiency of electricity supply compared to fuel conversion to process heat.

3) Assumed 200 percent efficiency of electricity input.

4) Heat.

5) Distribution losses 52 TWh (11 percent). Losses of peak power 23 TWh (15 GW fuel cells, 6 GW pumping power).

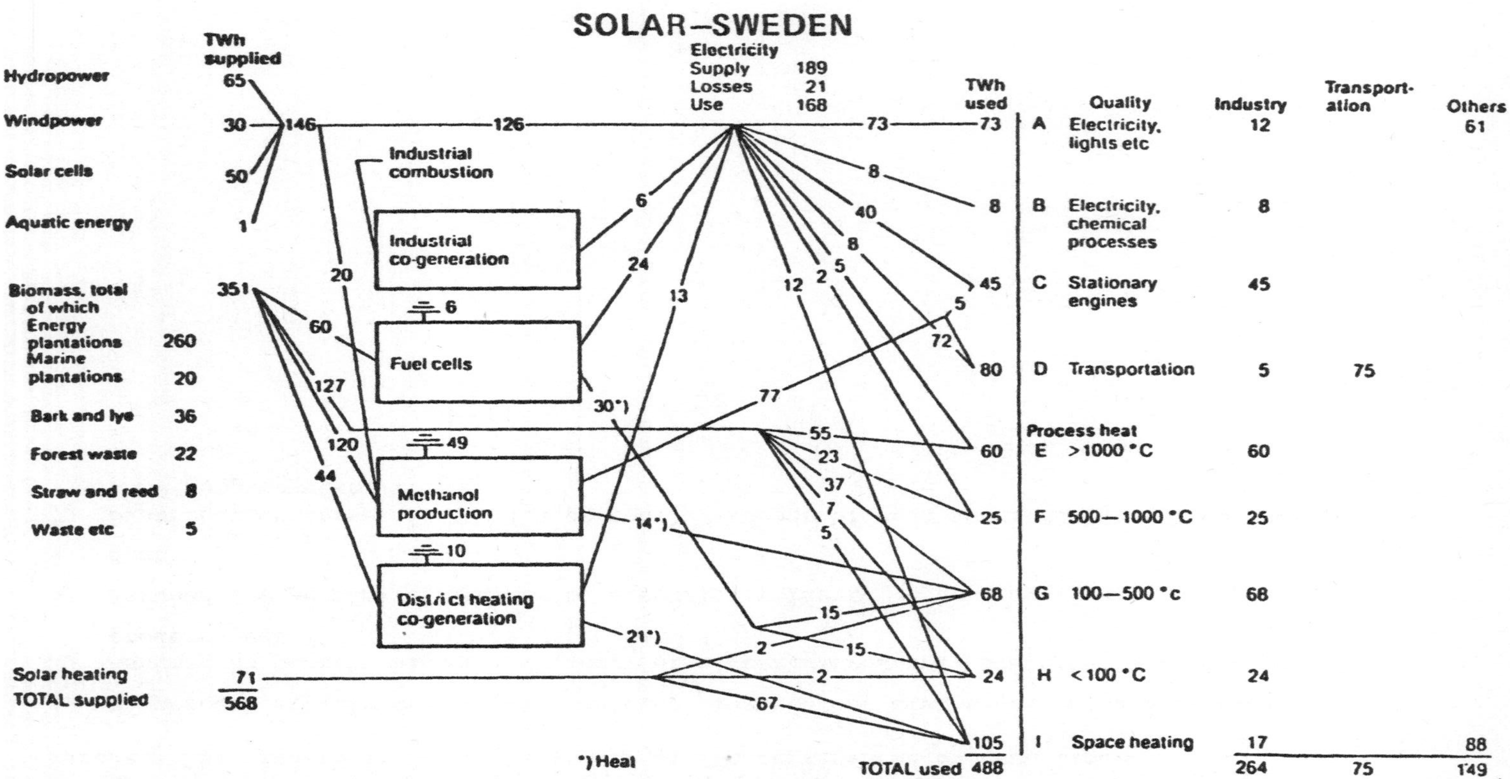

Figure 3. A renewable energy system in 2015. The supply of energy in the system is shown on the left; on the right is shown the energy consumption divided into different categories A–I of energy quality. The linkage between supply and consumption is shown in the middle. The figures indicate the number of TWh represented by each line.

ENERGY SUPPLY

Both Nuclear Sweden and Solar Sweden make use of the presently used indigenous energy sources. Hydropower is assumed to contribute 65 TWhe/year, which is slightly above the present level. Installations of a further 25-35 TWhe/year are technically and economically feasible but have so far been seen as too damaging environmentally and socially (1).

35 TWh of biomass (bark and lye) are presently used in the paper and pulp industry and is assumed to be used also in Solar and Nuclear Sweden.

A NUCLEAR SWEDEN YEAR 2015

In designing a uranium based energy system we have used technologies now available or planned by the nuclear industry. Light-water reactors (LWR) thus play a major role. However, since known high quality reserves of uranium in Sweden woild suffice for only 30 years operation of a large scale nuclear program based on LWR (without uranium and plutonium recycling) more uranium efficient fuel cycles have to be used. Breeder reactors of the type now under intensive development in several countries have therefore been introduced. The full fuel cycle is also assumed to be established in Sweden (although pilot studies about reprocessing have been conducted in the past, no present studies or plans exist for the fuel cycle).

The main energy carrier to the industrial, commercial and domestic sectors will be electricity, supplied mainly from 67 1.0-GWe-size nuclear power stations. Peak load is supplied by pumped storage and fuel cells. District heating is assumed for the larger metropolitan areas from six reactors of 1 GWe-size operated in co-generation and an additional 10 smaller reactors for heat production only. This saturates the possibilities for nuclear based district heating. Transportation is based on methanol or hydrogen (used, for example, in fuel cells). The system is shown in figure 2 and the components listed in Table 3 together with estimated costs. Breeder reactors are introduced in the year 2000.

Uncertainties in the Nuclear Sweden outline include technical and environmental issues, land use and political controversy. Technically, prototypes of breeder reactors are being built in other countries. Lisencing requirements, and therefore costs, are still very uncertain. Reprocessing technology is in an early stage of industrialization and has yet to be demonstrated on a commercial scale. The reprocess-

Table 3. Cost estimates used for components in Nuclear-Sweden (price levels at the turn of the year 1977/78) and in Swedish crowns, Mkr = million crowns (1 US$ = 4,40 Skr; 100 öre = 1 Skr).

		Capacity	Investment Costs	Operating Costs
Uranium mines	Ranstad mine 1300 tons of U/year plus 10 smaller mines of 400 tons/year	5200 tons of uranium/year	1.7 Mkr/year and ton[1]	260 kr/kg of natural uranium
Enrichment	A Swedish plant by 1990	3.6 M SWU	2115 kr/SWU year	300 kr/SWU
Fuel fabrication	LWR FBR			600 kr/kg enriched U 5000 kr/kg of fuel
Reactors	LWR	37 of 1000 MW electricity	3500 kr/kW 4375 kr/kW[2]	0.7 öre/kWh+45 kr/kW year
	FBR	36 of 1000 MW electricity	5250 kr/kW 6500 kr/kW[2]	"–
	Nuclear heating stations	10 of 200 MW	2000 kr/kW[2]	"–
Reprocessing	LWR fuel FBR fuel	2x1100 tons 360 tons	10 Mkr/year & ton 30 Mkr/year & ton	0.85 Mkr/year & ton 2.55 Mkr/year & ton

Table 3, continued

		Capacity	Investment Costs	Operating Costs
Waste isolation	Waste from 1500 tons U/year, corresponding to one repository of 10^4 KBS-size cannisters every 6 years[3]	As for reprocessing	3.1 Mkr/year & ton	0.1 Mkr/ton
Distribution	5000 km of 800 kV transmission, plus lower voltage lines	340 TWh	0.25 kr/annual kWh	-kr
Hydrogen production		45.5 GW	550 kr/kW	4% of annual investment
Pumped storage		6 GW	800 kr/kW	"-
Fuel cells		15 GW	2000 kr/kW	"-

[1]Costs are taken from various Swedish studies, referenced in detail in Solar Versus Nuclear: Choosing Energy Futures.

[2]Underground siting in rock; 75 percent of the reactors are assumed to be sited underground.

[3]As proposed by the Swedish Nuclear Fuel Safety Project.

Table 4. A Solar Sweden, Year 2015[1]

	Installed Capacity by 2051	Investment Costs	Operating Costs
Wind power	15 GW	4000 kr/kWh	2% of annual investment*
Solar cells	(50 GW) 500 km^2	ca. 2.5 kr/W (peak) plus 100 kr/m^2 installation, total 400 kr/m^2	2% of annual investment*
Solar heating	71 TWh/year	2 kr/annual kWh	2% of annual investment*
Methanol production	16 Mton (77 TWh)	1100 Mkr/750,000 tons per year	4% of annual investment*
Pump storage plant	15 GW	800 kr/kW	4% of annual investment*
Fuel cells	8 GW	2000 kr/kW	4% of annual investment*
Biomass			
Energy forest plantation	260 TWh/year		300 kr/ton dry weight
Other biomass (excluding bark and lyes)	55 TWh/year		230 kr/ton dry weight

*For maintenance and service.

[1]Costs are taken from various Swedish studies, referenced in detail in Solar Versus Nuclear: Choosing Energy Futures.

ing of breeder fuel is at an even earlier stage. Swedish land use will include 10-20 new sites for reactors and space for a large additional transmission grid (800 kV).

A SOLAR SWEDEN YEAR 2015 (3)

The solar energy influx in Sweden is 800-1000 kWh/m^2 annually. The potential for wind energy, biomass production and solar heating is rather substantial. A possible supply system for the year 2015 matched to the same level of final use as in the nuclear case is described in Figure 3 and Table 4. The biomass contribution dominates, but other large contributions come from photovoltaics, hydropower, windpower and solar heating. Energy is delivered to end use as electricity, methanol, solid fuels (wood) and heated water at various temperatures.

Biomass is produced mainly on land but also in marine areas. Recent research carried out in Sweden indicate a yield of 100-200 MWh per hectare per year (1 hectare = 10^4 m^2), in small, carefully managed areas planted with selected willow (Salix sp.) and poplar (Populus sp.) species. The average yield is likely to be lower as more realistic large-scale conditions are achieved. Further research, however, may also increase the maximum yield above the present preliminary results.

Energy plantations are assumed to contribute as much as 280 TWh requiring 2.9 million hectares at an average yield of 90 MWh/hectare per year. This land area is large, roughly of the same size as now used for agriculture. It is 6-7 per cent of Sweden's total land area. It is, however, much less than the 23 million hectares presently used for ordinary forestry supplying the paper and pulp industry.

Solar heating contributes 71 TWh per year, mostly for space heating. Heat has to be stored seasonally in district heating systems using low temperature heat and, for example, large reservoirs of water or direct storage in the ground. A number of pilot projects for this technology are now under way.

District heating using cogeneration plants with biomass for heat and electricity production is important for heating the larger cities.

Windpower is expected to contribute 30 TWh/year using 3700 units of 4 MW installed capacity in areas of Sweden with median wind speeds at the 50 or 100 meter level above 6 m/s. A large demonstration program is under way.

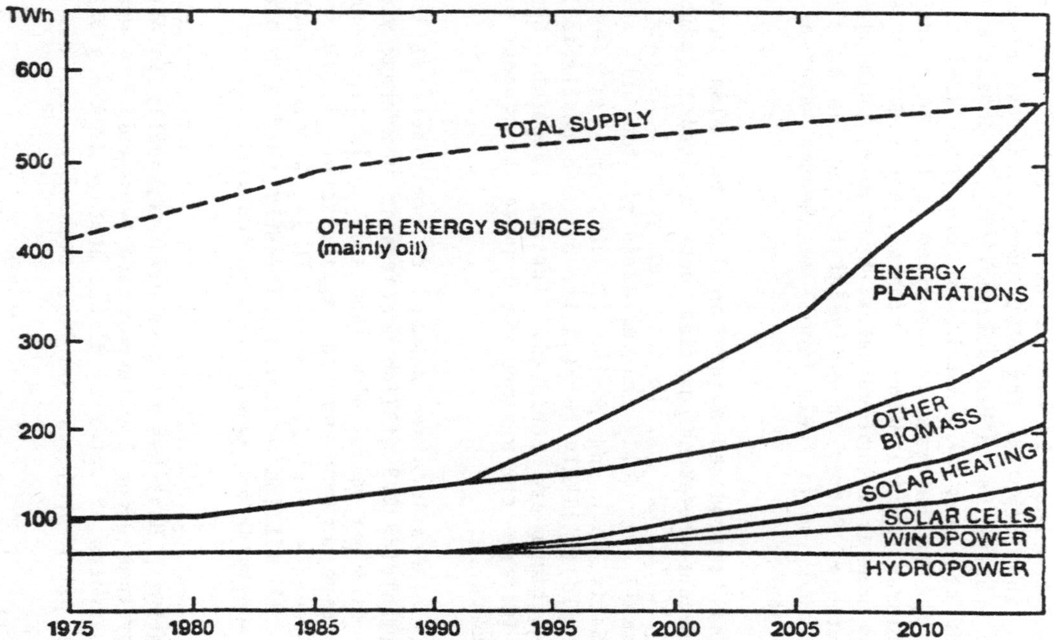

Figure 4. Contributions of renewable energy forms to energy supply in Solar Sweden. The broken line shows the assumed development of energy demand, which is close to the National Industrial Board's (SIND) forecast up to 1995 and thereafter increases more slowly.

Solar photovoltaic cells, in the order of 50 m^2/capita, located on roofs and walls, could be used in various ways. They could be directly connected to the load or used for the production of methanol (with biomass as feedstock) which may be a way to provide seasonal storage.

Fuel cells play an essential role both in the electricity system and in the transport sector. Methanol is used as fuel in the transportation sector. A large fraction of the cars and trucks are assumed to be powered by electric engines, either through fuel cells or electric batteries.

As in the nuclear system, uncertainties in several areas require extensive R&D efforts before any major commitment to the solar option can be made. In particular, the success of energy plantations and solar heating and storage is crucial. The environmental effects of energy plantations are presently not well understood and limitations may come from nutrient leaching, insect attacks, diseases, or land use competition. Solar cells are still much too costly to be considered although costs are expected to drop rapidly. The public acceptability of large scale wind energy is unknown.

The implementation rates assumed for the 1990s are somewhat lower than those considered possible by the National Board for Energy Source Development. The contribution of renewable energy sources is now around 25% and is not assumed to increase much until the 90s (see Figure 4). Large efforts are needed in the 80s to facilitate the rapid expansion of renewable energy after 1990.

COMPARISONS BETWEEN THE TWO SYSTEMS

The main object of these studies, it has to be stressed again, is not to make long term predictions but rather to analyse the requirements of a medium term energy policy designed not to foreclose any of the long term options. Such an analysis has to be based on a rather detailed study of the similarities and differences between the options.

No technical reason exists why the two systems could not be combined. However, a number of economic and (above all) institutional factors, some of which are addressed later, would probably lead to a dominant role for one or the other of the two systems.

Areas of uncertainty are large in both cases. Technologically, there seem to be uncertainties about the performance of fast breeder reactors (FBR) and reprocessing of FBR-fuel as well as over several solar technologies. The environmental impacts are potentially large, but different, in both cases. These, and other uncertainties about economics, are important reasons for not foreclosing either of the two options at present.

Economically the two alternatives seem to be (by the use of the cost estimates in Tables 3 and 4) roughly equivalent, although the uncertainties obviously are large. This result is based on a calculation of the total amount of resources needed to implement and operate the alternative energy system from 1990 to 2015. The total costs are between two and three times as large as today's. However, given conventional assumptions of economic growth, this increase in the cost of energy is compatible with a higher material standard of living.

If annual labor productivity increases by 2% overall, and by 5% in goods production, the doubling of the total Swedish economy assumed by the year 2015 is compatible with an increase in the cost of energy by a factor 2 or 3. Costs are not uniform, however. The cost of electricity is higher in the solar system than in the nuclear system. By the same token, however, the cost of nuclear systems may be higher for providing low temperature heat.

The main conclusion of this economic comparison is: when today's uncertainties are taken into account, it is too early to state that any of the alternatives are more economical than the others. A second conclusion is that neither of them needs to be a major obstacle to increasing the material standard of living.

Technically, the systems imply large differences in the choice of energy carriers and distribution systems. The way present systems are designed will therefore have important effects on later costs of connecting new supply sources.

It takes decades to establish large district heating systems. Thus, present policy on district heating operating characteristics (such as design temperatures) have to be adjusted in order to facilitate the later introduction of solar heating. In the same way, policies with respect to direct electric space-heating will have to be adjusted.

Industrial energy use differs considerably between the alternatives. In the nuclear case, electricity is used for process heat while, in the solar case, direct combustion of biomass would supply the heat. Obviously, the equipment necessary for these two end-uses would differ greatly and ways have to be found to reconcile the differences.

Electricity production in Solar Sweden is located closer to the user, is less predictable (wind and solar) and is more frequently connected to co-use of waste-heat than in Nuclear Sweden. It thus requires different load management practices.

In sum, the technical differences are large. Future freedom of action on the supply side requires that distribution and end-use systems are developed so that different supply alternatives can be connected in the future. This poses problems of institutional adaptation which may well be more important than the economic and technical aspects of the alternative systems.

Institutional differences. The large technical differences noted above imply large institutional consequences depending on the choice of energy system. A nuclear Sweden can only be implemented through a strong central authority - not only the fuel cycle but also the total electricity supply system has to be controlled by central authority. Locations for fuel cycle components, reactors and transmission lines have to be based on national decisions, implying that local authorities will have to give up their present right to veto siting decisions.

Solar Sweden, on the other hand, requires more integration between end-use, distribution and supply. Land-use planning for buildings, biomass plantations and wind energy have to be developed and implemented.

Thus, it seems that both the nuclear and the solar case will imply increased public planning. The nuclear case cannot be implemented without strengthening the planning on the centralized, national level and the solar case cannot be implemented without giving more power to both local and central authorities.

Other differences are to be found in the capital market which will have very different roles in Nuclear and Solar Sweden. In the former, the typical recipient (or customer) is the national government or a large utility; in the latter, a large number of individuals, small firms, local authorities, regional and central governments, are the customers.

The overall conclusion is that the social organization, in particular the institutional infrastructure, differs very much between the two cases. Thus, the medium term energy policy has to be directed towards establishing institutions that, in an overall sense, are unbiased towards different technologies. This is no small task in itself.

IMPLICATIONS FOR MEDIUM-TERM ENERGY POLICY

It is now possible to combine the medium and the longer term perspectives. A number of studies of the medium term supply show - and this has also been the conclusion of various large political majorities - that nuclear power should not be rejected in this medium term perspective. The government Bill of March 1979 indicated that the present nuclear program of 12 reactors, together with some more hydropower, co-generation of electricity, conservation and possible wind power, is sufficient to satisfy electricity demand through end of the century. Also, oil could, during the medium term, be replaced in part by other energy sources, such as wood, natural gas, peat and coal. However, the long term studies also show that a medium term policy, apart from securing supply for the medium term, has to include specific steps designed to create freedom of action in the longer term.

CONTROLLING THE MOMENTUM

During the last 20-30 years, the accepted vision by all political parties, industry and the electric utilities has been to increase the use of nuclear power. R&D has been strongly oriented in this direction, in Sweden as well as internationally (4). A reactor industry in need of further orders, the organization of the electricity distribution system, the expectations that have underlain the planning in different sectors of society - these, and other factors together, build up a momentum towards a continuously expanding role for nuclear energy. If the call for freedom of action outlined above as a necessary component of the medium term energy policy is to be taken seriously, the mechanisms behind the momentum have to be controlled and, therefore, identified.

One such set of mechanisms has to do with a forecast <u>overcapacity</u> during the 80s in the electric supply sector. In fact, the Swedish power industry used a similar overcapacity during the 60s to discourage cogeneration by industries and local authorities (5). This overcapacity makes the utility sector and the nuclear industry negative to all measures which tend to reduce demand for electricity and it also makes investments in other supply alternatives (for example, combined generation) very uncertain. There is a related and marked tendency among utilities to advocate end-use patterns that are highly inflexible, such as direct electric resistance space-heating, thus ensuring the market for nuclear generated electricity (roughly half of the nuclear program for 1990 is in fact to be used for electric space-heating purposes). Without electric space heating, it would hardly have been possible to establish an indigenous Swedish nuclear reactor industry.

Another set of mechanisms tends to favor electrification over other secondary energy carriers. This, again, is most notable in the space-heating market. The medium term alternative to electric space-heating is district heating, both in newly constructed buildings and when the oil-based furnaces in existing buildings are replaced. This district heating could be produced by different fuels either in large or small plants. District heating is favored by many local authorities. It does not, however, have the same privileged status on the capital market as electricity supply.

A third set of mechanisms favors large-scale, utility-operated electricity production over small scale and dispersed production, regardless of whether it is done by local authorities in combined generation plants or by industries or through other means. Partly, this is again dependent on how the capital market works, but it also depends on the power to determine existing principles of rate-setting. As long as these reflect the cost structure of utilities they tend to create barriers towards dispersed electricity production and conservation.

A fourth set of mechanisms is related to the conditions under which local authorities work. Many long-term solar technologies and those medium term distribution systems that make solar competitive in the long term require considerably more planning by the local authorities than most of them are yet capable of. Moreover, the financial situation of local authorities in Sweden has to be improved, but this will require considerable legislative work simply because of the interdependence of different rules systems. The present situation favors either technologies that fit well into existing rules or those that are being pushed by very powerful entrepreneurs. Wind power, solar heating, cogeneration, fuel cells, photovoltaics, heat pumps and many other technologies close to the consumer may pose serious threats to the existing utilities' plans for expanding base-load in general and nuclear plants in particular. Differences in lead times tend to reinforce these problems.

In a system that has already invested in nuclear plants, electric utilities will have to set rates that protect existing investments and, consequently, dissuade consumers and local authorities from investing in more dispersed technologies for producing and conserving electricity. The Swedish federation of electric distributors has considered rates for electric heat pumps that have special penalties for peak power demand. These rates would depress the market for the heat pump industries. The rates could be set in such a way as to stimulate these and other dispersed solar technologies but they would then reduce the market for the nuclear technologies.

Measures to create a solar industry therefore threaten the nuclear industry. Conversely, measures to protect the nuclear industry and thus the demand for nuclear generated electricity may very well create an insurmountable barrier for a nascent solar industry.

Steps that ensure long term flexibility are thus likely to challenge short and medium term industrial policy as well as threaten medium term financial stability of today's utilities. The reconciliations and balancing of these conflicts is therefore one of the primary aims of a medium term energy policy.

A policy attuned to "freedom of action" must therefore cover broad areas. Under the Swedish conditions, some of the main points would be:

<u>Strengthening the local authorities</u> in the field of energy. Many local authorities are today in charge of the distribution of electricity and the production and distribution of district heating. This responsibility should be mandatory for all local authorities. They should also be responsible for conservation of energy. Moreover, the local authorities should be encouraged to become as self reliant in energy as possible.

<u>Regulatory and financial reform</u> of the energy sector in order to ensure adequate financing on the local level and also ensuring that the rate structure stimulates conservation and implementation of dispersed and capital intensive supply alternatives. This reform should also include financing of conservation efforts and require that the balancing of conservation and supply is done explicitly and on the local level. Technical design parameters, which now are almost exclusively the responsibility of professional organizations, should also become subject to political scrutiny (with subsequent regulation as well as some deregulation).

<u>Increased control of large scale energy users</u> by the national government, both processing industry and local authorities. The main aim is to ensure that markets are established for production of biomass and that end-use and conversion devices are compatible with several supply alternatives. Conservation programs for these users should be monitored by the national government.

<u>State-financed development and procurement of new energy technology</u> is an important tool for creating incentives for

industry to establish it in new markets. This should cover technologies in space-heating, transports, but also small scale electricity production etc., where local and central governments could become large consumers.

Land-use planning, in order to ensure that land is available for reactor sites, biomass plantations, wind energy plants, solar heating stations, ite. This requires a combination of local and central initiatives.

Electric utility reform in order to encourage the introduction of more dispersed electric technologies. This can be done through giving local authorities exclusive right of distribution and divest bulk transport (the grid above say 130 kV) from production interests. The bulk transport utility (which should be publicly controlled and preferably owned) would function as a wholesale broker and can introduce such rates that distributors are encouraged to channel their investments into alternatives to large base-load plants.

There is no question that this kind of a program is rather controversial. Circumstances could, of course, be imagined where these types of interventions are not necessary - particularly if the nuclear option is convincingly demonstrated and accepted as superior. The imperative, as we see it, is to establish a policy for the case when genuine uncertainty still remains large.

Some discussions on solar and nuclear futures have centered around the theme centralization and decentralization. It should be evident by the above presentation that a policy directed towards a Solar Sweden does not seem to reduce the need for central authority and planning.

Moreover, the challenge that an open-ended energy policy poses to a policy maker can hardly be stressed enough. Pressures to take decisions and make commitments will be very strong from both constituencies favoring a particular long-term option. A flexible policy could be seen as a way to handle and thus reduce overall uncertainty for governments and the public at large, but it has exactly the opposite effect on those groups and industries that already are committed. Their uncertainty is increased by the very same policy.

A policy aiming at flexibility will require a balance of interests, which in turn means more control by the national government; in fact, much more than the policy required for a clear-cut implementation of either a Solar or a Nuclear case. But that can be seen as the price that has to be paid in order to have a democratic freedom of choice.

REFERENCES

Detailed list of references (mainly in Swedish) can be found in "Solar versus Nuclear: Choosing Energy Futures" published by Pergamon Press, Oxford, England, December 1979, and in references 3 and 5.

1. Energy policy decision in Parliament 1975 and numerous later statements of political leaders. Current Sweden, The Swedish Institute.

2. Lee Shipper, A.J. Lichtenberg, Efficient Energy Use and Well-Being. The Swedish Example, Science, Vol. 194 (1976), p. 1001.

3. Thomas B. Johansson & Peter Steen, Solar Sweden (Secretariat for Futures Studies, Stockholm, 1977). Thomas B. Johansson & Peter Steen, Solar Sweden, Ambio, Vol. 7, No. 2 (1978), pp. 70-74. The Bulletin of Atomic Scientists, Vol. 35 (October 1979), pp. 19-22.

4. Erik Moberg, Forskning, utveckling och demonstration inom energiomradet - en global oversikt 1978 (DFE Report No. 12, Energy Research and Development Commission, Stockholm, 11978). (Swedish).

5. Måns Lonnroth, Thomas B. Johansson & Peter Steen, Energy in Transition (Secretariat for Futures Studies, Stockholm, 1977). California University Press, Los Angeles, 1980.